THE C... C...O...M... ...RD H... ...OOK

Shuttleworth College Learning Resources

Tel: 01234 291020

This book is due for return on or before the last date shown below.

WITHDRAWN

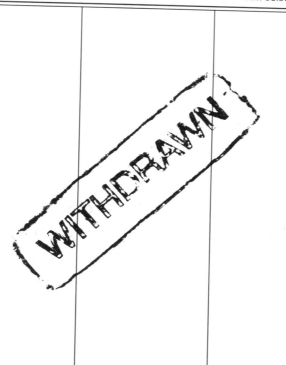

D1426037

THE
CLASSIC OUTBOARD MOTOR HANDBOOK

Peter Hunn

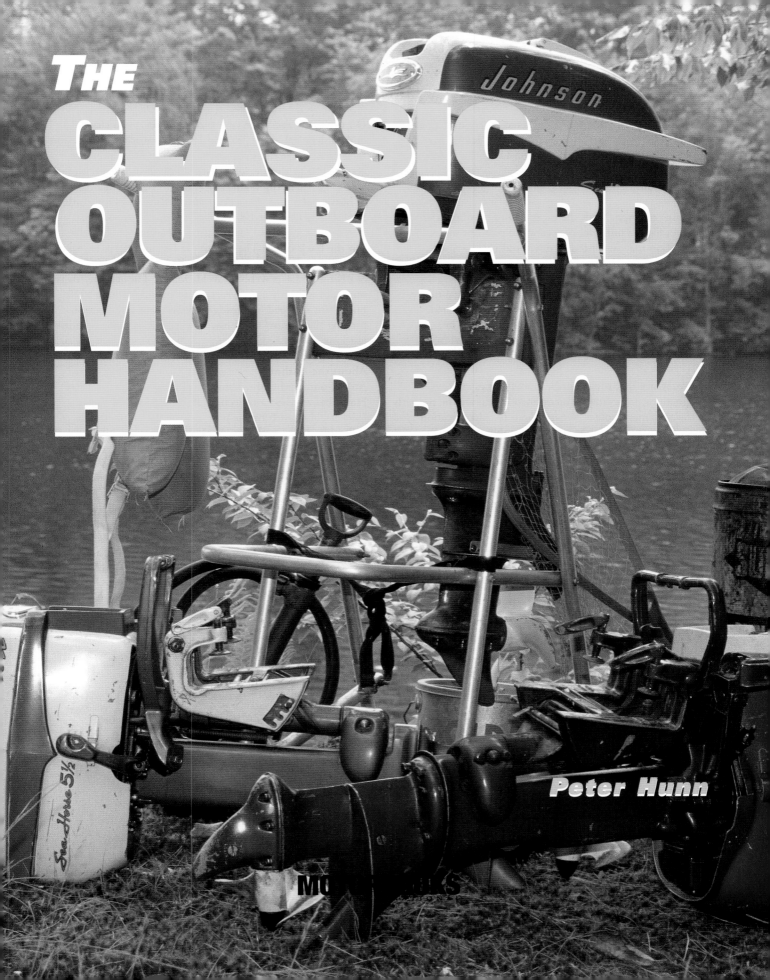

MOTORBOOKS

First published in 2003 by Motorbooks International, an inprint of MBI Publishing Company, 380 Jackson Street, Suite 200, St. Paul, MN 55101-3885 USA

© Peter Hunn, 2003

All rights reserved. With the exception of quoting brief passages for the purposes of review, no part of this publication may be reproduced without prior written permission from the Publisher.

The information in this book is true and complete to the best of our knowledge. All recommendations are made without any guarantee on the part of the author or Publisher, who also disclaim any liability incurred in connection with the use of this data or specific details.

We recognize that some words, model names and designations, for example, mentioned herein are the property of the trademark holder. We use them for identification purposes only. This is not an official publication.

Motorbooks International books are also available at discounts in bulk quantity for industrial or sales-promotional use. For details write to Special Sales Manager at Motorbooks International Wholesalers & Distributors, 380 Jackson Street, Suite 200, St. Paul, MN 55101-3885 USA

ISBN 0-7603-1552-3

On the front cover: A freshly restored Mercury Mark 25 Hurricane with colorful, two-tone Merchromatic covers awaits her second "maiden" voyage. A few months before this image was shot, our beautiful 1956 cover model looked much worse than even the Merc 25 on page 10. *Dave Dayger*

On the title page: Take your pick! Members of a classic-outboarder's stable of 1957 and 1958 Johnson Sea Horses wait their turns at the transom. This trio cost the buff a total of about $150 to acquire at swap meets, but it took a labor of love to get them running. They represent motors he dreamed of owning as a teen. *From Peter Hunn's* Beautiful Outboards *published by Devereux Books (www.devereuxbooks.com)*

On the back cover: The author's father, at age 10, enjoys a stint at the tiller of an Evinrude-built Montgomery Ward's Sea King on Lake Webb in Weld, Maine. Though the trusty outboard was only a few years old when this August 1939 photo was snapped, it already appeared rather shopworn, proving that "mint" or "showroom" condition usually didn't last long.

About the Author

An old-outboard enthusiast since elementary school, Peter Hunn has amassed a collection of more than 200 classic "kickers," but with the help of his wife has thinned his collection down to about 75. He has been a contributor to the Antique Outboard Motor Club's quarterly magazine and has authored four previous books on the subject: *Beautiful Outboards, The Golden Age of Outboard Racing, The Vintage Culture of Outboard Racing,* and *The Old Outboard Book,* now in its third edition. Mr. Hunn lives in Upstate New York, where he teaches media and communications studies at Baldwinsville Central School District and at the State University of New York–Oswego.

Edited by Dennis Pernu
Designed by Chris Fayers

Printed in China

CONTENTS

DEDICATION

For my dad, the Reverend John Hunn, who in addition to gently shepherding souls has a sixth sense about revitalizing ailing mechanical items. I gave him one of the earliest copies of my previous work, *The Old Outboard Book*, even though he prefers trying to figure out how to put things back together without being prompted by a text. *The Classic Outboard Motor Handbook* is also dedicated to the memory of my grandfather, Edward Hunn, Ph.D. I imagine him jotting down notes while quietly enjoying this volume, and then taking great delight in showing me how several steps in the motor repair chapters might have been streamlined.

INTRODUCTION

Although at the time I'd just learned to print a few basic words in big block letters, the idea of writing this book came to me in first grade. That's mostly because I liked to daydream, possessed an active imagination, really loved boating, and was tightly grasping a promise my father had made. He said we could buy an outboard motor if I could find one for $25 or less. Actually, that represented pretty decent dough in 1960, especially for someone on a 75-cent weekly allowance. Compounding this conundrum, a local marina guy warned me, "Your average second-hand $25 'kicker' probably needs 50 bucks' worth of parts and repairs . . . plus a special order technical booklet."

Downcast, I trudged from the ship's store to a nearby dock, sat at the end, chin in hand, and concocted plans to find an orphaned outboard or two and learn to fix them myself. In retrospect, this brainstorm was akin to a kid who'd only hit a couple of baseballs picturing his victorious face in the Sunday paper's sports pages.

Happily, I got one of those low-budget motors—in fact, a battered 1928 Johnson Model A-35 for only $15—and proceeded to dismantle it. Scores of others followed, along with a lifelong fascination with vintage outboards. This title is one of about a half-dozen I've enjoyed writing on the topic of old kickers. Rather than attempting to conform to a strict shop manual format, *The Classic Outboard Motor Handbook* endeavors to share information, experience, observations, suggestions, and actual case studies by walking you through the adventures of several old engine restoration projects. Luckily, not all of these revitalizations took a predictable route. There were a few instances, for example, when our initial powerhead rebuilds presented more methodical mystery than quick success, sending us back to the proverbial drawing board. Perhaps you'll agree, however, that the resultant tales of additional sleuthing to arrest the real culprits add to this work's intended spirit: to encourage you to get your vintage outboard purring.

Readers without an old motor need not worry. This book also offers tips on finding a promising motor to redo and use for a fraction of the cost of a new outboard.

THE ALLURE OF CLASSIC OUTBOARDING

In 1972, Johnson Motors celebrated its 50th anniversary by cosponsoring an Antique Outboard Motor Club meet at a suburban Chicago-area marina. The assembled multitude of old outboards and enthusiasts was especially significant because it was the first such event with a national focus. Rows upon rows of engines on display and the happy spectacle of vintage kickers busily buzzing boats through the marina's harbor provided more than ample reason for positive public attention. Senior citizens smiled at the memories that the World War I–vintage staccato motor music instantly generated. Middle-aged folks ruefully remarked about their first outboard being "just like that classic blue '53 Evinrude." Kids on the dock excitedly hinted about maybe getting a ride in the boat powered by "the funny little silver motor with the rudder." When scenes of the meet were broadcast on Chicago TV news programs, additional onlookers flocked to the venue the next day. More than a few got the classic-outboard bug and subsequently

Johnson Motors' 50th anniversary proved a seminal event for the then-fledgling Antique Outboard Motor Club and the classic-outboarding hobby. Here's a candid shot of the "pits" taken shortly before the 1972 meet officially opened. Word of mouth and broadcast coverage soon attracted a capacity crowd of spectators eager to observe the vintage motors operating near this docking area.

Likely suspects in a typical vintage outboard flea market. Most are offered as "project motors," while the restored Chris-Craft 10-horse Commander advertises what the others could become with a winter of dedication.

snapped up an old motor to revitalize and enjoy using. Today, the then-new 1972 engines that were displayed alongside vintage machines at that Illinois marina can be considered "old."

Whether one likes such "modern antiques" or has a heart for even older outboards, there's ample opportunity for gaining technical knowledge and skills, building an interesting collection, completing a rewarding parent/child project, running a vintage engine, showing off in front of boaters with brand-new $10,000 motors, and enjoying lots of priceless old-fashioned family fun. Most folks new to the classic-outboard hobby simply need some basic information to get things started. First and foremost is being able to recognize what you're looking for in an old motor. There are still amazing numbers of reasonably priced "experienced engines" available through garage sales, on-line auctions (watch out for those sometimes wildly high e-prices!), boat shops, coworkers, neighbors, and Antique Outboard Motor Club meets.

Identification tags on most outboards from the 1940s onward can be found on locations such as the side of the transom bracket, between thumbscrews, on the motor leg, or affixed to the steering-handle bracket. Many pre–World War II open-flywheel motors are identified on their flywheel-mounted rope sheave plates, but some have tags, too. Look first for the model designation, and then serial number.

This Truman-era Evinrude Sportsman would make a good project motor if it had its bottom half. So, maybe the $15 asking price is no true bargain. A classic outboarder without a ready parts source would probably never get this kicker back on the water.

The sign says it's a "classic," but sans its carburetor, rewind starter, fuel tank, shrouding, and propeller, even at $10 this deal stinks, unless one has access to those parts. It also appears that a chunk of aluminum is missing from the powerhead's emergency rope sheave.

The author in the 1970s, smiling after his purchase of an uncommon Voyager by Champion Outboard. A decade later, he traded the motor—still minus its lower unit—to a collector who had that crucial part.

Where ya gonna find one? The non-threaded plastic fuel tank caps used on a few Evinrude models for a couple of years are often long gone when the engines hit the flea market. The buff who bought this motor forgot to check for the cap until he got home. Check over the motor before making the deal. Sometimes, missing parts can be rather easily replaced or workable substitutes found.

IDENTIFYING VINTAGE OUTBOARDS

"Hey, my brother-in-law has an old motor just like that!" an intrigued passerby declared after noticing a rare 1930 racing outboard on exhibition at a boat show. The fellow's relative lived about two hours away from me, but his lead could have been well worth pursuing. Turned out, though, that the displayed limited-production, high-speed model's alleged "double" was actually a 1965 British Seagull, a low-power motor built with Depression-era design and appearance. The guy's complete misdiagnosis demonstrates that unless one has more than a passing interest in vintage outboards—or "old iron" as some buffs say—it can be a bit of a challenge to determine a motor's exact pedigree.

While this volume is meant as a repair and revitalization reference, rather than a historical treatise, documentation of a kicker's identity and lineage is also crucial when seeking parts and technical advice. Many are the Saturday mornings I've visited the local marina when someone stopped by for the most basic of outboard parts, say, a shear pin. Typically, the customer offers little more description than "It's for an old Evinrude 5-horse or something . . . maybe early 1960s?" I've stepped in to help, admittedly sometimes completely confusing the issue, by asking about the motor's color or some other hopefully identifying characteristic. More than once these sessions became livelier than a game of charades, but yielded no definitive results. It need not turn out that way. The key to identification success is gathering the following *before* beginning one's restoration project:

- Motor maker's name
- Model name or number
- Serial number
- Horsepower
- Year built (This is best determined by comparing the brand, model, and serial numbers with service manual charts, *The Old Outboard Book,* or another chronological roster.)

Unfortunately, across the several hundred outboard brands manufactured in the United States alone since the early 1900s, there is no universal spot on which to look for a motor's enumeration. Decals on the integral fuel tank (as opposed to one of those red, remote tanks) and shroud-mounted emblems are handily observable, unless worn off by age, sunlight, gas, or general abuse. For engines with exposed flywheels (often characteristic of pre–World War II models), ID marks are typically found on the rope sheave or starter plate. Some makers stamped a corresponding serial number on the crankcase, too. Matching numbers thus ensure that the rope sheave is original and consequently confirm that its model designation is correct.

"Modern" (post–World War II) outboards were frequently tagged on the motor driveshaft "leg" housing or on a small sheet metal plate riveted to the transom bracket somewhere between the thumbscrews. Stamped identification tags are the most readable, although many imprints were wimpy and difficult to make out. Some tags or stickers have painted or screen-printed lettering, and both can be highly susceptible to fading or chipping. The printed plate on a Scott-Atwater 16 comes to mind. Anxious to determine whether or not this uncommon model was Scott's first-year 16, I squirted the ID with some parts cleaner and gave a quick rub with a shop rag. The writing instantly wiped off and with it all hope of definitive dating.

Shall I Buy This Old Motor?

Don't believe that any engine with a "For Sale" sign runs well unless you're running it.

There's no need to pay big money for the average old outboard. Consider them all "average" until you feel you can tell the common engines from the rare ones. In the former category, there are still lots to go around at reasonable prices. And be wary of those sometimes unrealistically high on-line auction bids for vintage engines. See the price guide in *The Old Outboard Book* (available through Classic Motorbooks and www.motorbooks.com), or contact Antique Outboard Motor Club members on-line (www.aomci.org) for advice.

Salt is bad for cardiac patients, old outboards, and classic motor restorers. The heavy white corrosion on this 1955 Evinrude Super Fastwin 15 is an outward sign of much needed attention for exterior and internal parts. In fact, seawater ate through some of this poor mill's water jackets, clogged much of the rest of its cooling system, and caused the subsequently overheated powerhead to seize up. That masking tape on the motor's rewind was labeled "FREE," and before the end of the day, it left the swap meet with folks willing to try their hands at stripping it.

A Mercury Mark 25, seen here for sale in a Connecticut basement, has signs of saltwater "acne" on its shrouds. The brownish line midway up its lower unit indicates that the motor was likely left moored in the water when the boat to which it was attached wasn't in use. It's also a good bet that this 1956 Merc's water jackets suffer from salt deposits. Because this model provides some access to these cooling jackets, they can be cleaned, but it's not a quick fix. Note the test wheel in place of a propeller; it's for full-speed (reduced turbulence) running in a test tank.

Beware of dismantled motors reputed to be "all in the box." This classic "basket case" turned out to contain parts from three different outboard brands, along with a lawnmower tire and a trailer stoplight!

Kicker Tips 1.2

A Great First Project Motor

"Simple, but well-engineered" are useful watchwords when seeking that first project outboard. Criteria include not only a good overall mechanical design, but also a track record that proves the motor was and is reliable in a wide variety of user applications. While almost every experienced classic-outboard buff can happily come up with a list of favorite firsts, a great universal candidate is the 1.5-horse Gale Products single. Thousands were sold from the late 1940s to early 1950s under names such as or including Buccaneer, Atlas-Royal, Hiawatha, and Sea Bee. In fact, many of the Evinrude/Johnson–produced, Gale-based kickers make a fine first revitalization project. The brand's generic qualities have kept their prices reasonable, and those qualities still make them a "quick read" for novices looking to acquire some mechanical skills.

Be it ever so humble, there's nothing like a basic Gale Products putt-putt. The 1948 and 1949 horse-and-a-half Goodyear Sea Bee had no lower shrouding, no rewind starter, nor anything else complex about her. Most every Sea Bee found with decent compression can be coaxed to spark and run. Full restorations only require a couple of colors of spray paint from the local auto parts store.

An exception to the rule. Although it might appear primitive, a realistically priced, very early outboard, even if missing parts, is often worth the extra effort and expense it takes to find components for its restoration. This circa 1908 Waterman vertical cylinder Porto represents a potential cornerstone engine for any serious buff's collection. Often, these pioneer motor projects take several years of hunting for parts and information, as well as the actual restoration work.

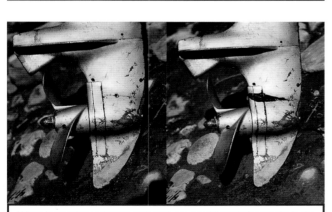

When inspecting a vintage outboard, search diligently for cracks in the castings, especially below the waterline. Long ago, water seeping into this Sea King's gearcase froze and cracked it (left). Although the crack appeared to be just a scratch, when the motor was brought home and grease was applied to the lower unit, the lubricant quickly made the break apparent (right). The owner decided to use the kicker anyway, and is OK doing so, as long as he refills the gearcase after every run.

Beware of using ether-based products on painted surfaces you'd like to preserve.

Armed with model names, letters, and/or numbers, though, the novice old-outboarder can begin researching his or her motor or one that's for sale. On second thought, jotting down motor ID information isn't just a matter for someone new to the classic hobby. There is still such a variety of vintage mills waiting to be discovered or in circulation that even the most experienced buffs occasionally uncover one that isn't readily identifiable. For both of these types of enthusiasts, I wrote *The Old Outboard Book* (available through Classic Motorbooks and www.motorbooks.com). Its model and year guide is designed to bring you up to speed on your motor's history, so you can speak the language often required when hunting for parts and seeking specific model information from other classic outboarders. It makes a good companion to this volume.

AVOIDING SOMEONE ELSE'S TROUBLE

Beginning with a bottom-line recommendation, I'll relay the good news about choosing which old outboard to buy.

Kicker Tips 1.3

Common Outboard Motor Deal Breakers

When pondering a classic-outboard purchase, be sure to check for these common deal breakers, which can be informally tested.

1. The outboard is shy some vital parts. Missing pieces can include anything from the carburetor to the steering handle. Unless it's an incredibly rare motor at a giveaway price (that you could use as trading stock), keep asking yourself, "Why do I need this one and where will I ever find the stuff this poor old mill needs?" Better yet, maybe you shouldn't consider it "the poor old" motor, as that sort of sentimentality often begins the process of breaking down common sense. Before you know it, you've got a garage full of partial engines. The more familiar you are with this particular model, the better able you'll be to recognize missing or wrongly retrofitted parts.

2. Not much on the motor moves. If the flywheel won't turn, it's typically a sure sign of seized bearings or pistons, or sometimes stuck lower-unit gears. The powerhead is usually the culprit, and is seldom an easy fix. Grasp the "speed" lever. If its associated magneto/timer plate won't budge, something ugly is going on.

3. Lots of rust, pitting, corrosion, or all three. Motors used in salt water, left outside, infested with critter nests, or stored in a damp place frequently exhibit these problematic symptoms of "restorer's heartache."

4. No spark. Sometimes this is caused by a bad condenser or dirty ignition points (both easily remedied), so it shouldn't always be considered a fatal flaw. Even so, the motor must have spark in order to run.

This late-1960s Mini-Motor sure is a cutie, but if missing some parts or ailing from, say, a cracked plastic gearcase, it might not bring much satisfaction to a novice classic outboarder unfamiliar with how to access replacement components for uncommon kickers.

Evinrude rowboat motor from about 1910. With various updates, these single-cylinder engines were offered for nearly two decades. Some collectors consider this basic Evinrude to be the antique outboard. Thousands were produced and some still turn up for sale. Models with battery ignition are the "easiest" to get running.

An Elto Speedster from 1929 goes for a test cruise soon after its revitalization. Most Speedsters from 1928 to 1931 make for nice project motors, as long as one can successfully service the Atwater-Kent ignition system that uses a 6-volt electric-fence battery to give the motor spark. Note the dark line on the fuel tank just to the left of the flywheel and those drips under the flywheel's right side. They were caused by oil that leaked past the top bearing where the crankshaft meets the crankcase. While the author had loads of fun that day, he got covered with oily "Elto spots."

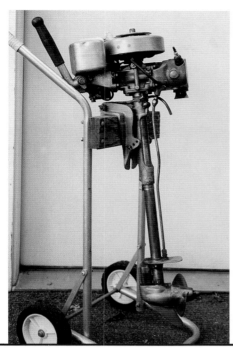

They might not look like much, but simple, low-horsepower 1930s fishing motors such this Evinrude-built Montgomery Ward Sea King single can be relatively easy to redo into a nicely running antique. The bronze lower unit on this model adds interest and "shine appeal."

Little kickers like the 1930s and 1940s Evinrude Sportwin have a reputation for running well and not being overly complex. This one is fitted with rewind starting and a "weedless" lower unit. Their relative abundance in antique outboarding circles keeps prices reasonable. Although they're not visible in this photo, oversized lawn tractor wheels were successfully adapted to this wheel stand by a buff who was tired of getting mired in the soft shoreline. A length of threaded rod for an axle, some washers, a couple of nuts, and a trip to the mower shop graveyard for bargain tires was all it took.

When buying an old motor from a non-enthusiast, be sure to ask questions like, "Do you have its owner's manual?" and "Might there still be some spare parts for it in the garage?" The collector who answered a local shopper-paper ad for a "real old and little boat motor" wondered if the seller had its starter rope. After a short search he was rewarded with not only the rope, but also the motor's official gas can kit and the footlocker that the 0.9-horsepower Scout came in.

The fact is that if you're careful not to pay much for an unrestored vintage kicker, even a lousy one can provide you with some educational benefit. In the 1950s, pleasure boating writer Bob Whittier pointed out that "many good outboard mechanics are self-taught. The obvious way to teach yourself is to buy a battered old outboard motor for $5 or $10, take it apart, put it together, run it, and tinker with it."

Some 50 years after Whittier's suggestion was first printed it still makes sense. After factoring inflation, his Sputnik-era pricing isn't too far from today's cost for such a clunker either. At virtually any Antique Outboard Motor Club swap meet, there are sure to be a few "restorable" engines for well under 100 bucks. (See details about such events online at www.aomci.org.) Toward the end of many of these sessions, deals from $15 to $50 are not uncommon. No matter the bargain factor, however, it's best to bring home a classic kicker that's as free of problems as possible. One summer as a youngster, I dragged several dozen "strays" into the basement. Although cheap, most were hopelessly incomplete, internally seized, or just plain worn out. And each one had some disorder that I had failed to detect when I enthusiastically decided to shell out the dough for it. Old-outboard acquisition reality number

As far as the eye can see, classic outboards awaiting new homes and new lives on the water represent just one section of several acres filled with old motors and parts. The small black Mercury near the photo's lower right was snapped up that day to serve as a project engine in this book.

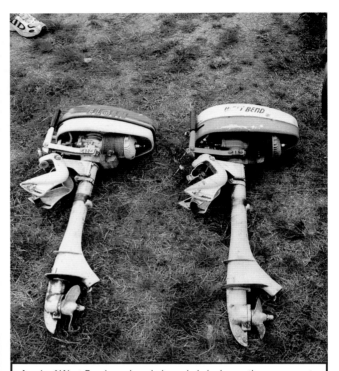

A pair of West Bend–produced air-cooled singles on the swap-meet field. The foot in the photo's upper left corner belongs to the wife of a new collector; she was trying to decide which of the $30 motors to buy for a family project for her "guys." Seconds later, she offered 40 bucks for both, and the seller happily loaded them into her SUV. Having a spare or "parts" motor is always a good idea. In this case, however, both were in good enough shape for revitalization.

It's a bit rusty, but a yank of the starter cord revealed decent compression and spark on this Firestone 3.6-horse single. Made in large quantities by Scott-Atwater, these generic kickers also came through with labels like Scott, McCulloch, and Wizard. While most buffs don't get overly excited about them, any denomination of this well-designed old outboard can provide a neat project and hours of fun afloat. One caveat: Avoid examples that have been used in saltwater.

Some enthusiasts like novelty outboards such as this 1980s Versatool chainsaw-to-lower unit setup. When closing the deal on unconventional kickers, be especially sure that all of the related parts and accessories are present.

Golden Jet 500

Eska's®

SLEEK, DEPENDABLE

4 H.P.

OUTBOARD

An effortless one-pull starter winds up the rugged Golden Jet 500. The instant-touch carburetor control quickly delivers the power to the propeller. The dependable power head is especially designed by Power Products . . . a division of Tecumseh Products Co. This thoroughly tested and proved engine means the ultimate in dependability.

A 5.1 cubic inch displacement engine delivers more useable power than any other engine the same size. It's air-cooled with a water-cooled leg . . . operates freely in freezing temperatures without damaging the engine. All submerged parts are rust-free aluminum as well as the smartly designed engine cowling. This all-weather outboard is ideal for duck hunters, fishermen or as an auxiliary motor.

Over 6,600 Lauson and Power Products service stations ideally located for fast, efficient service.

● **Industry rated at 4 H.P.**
● **An easy carrying 29 pounds**
● **Automatic rewind starter**
● **360-degree steering for easy handling**
● **An aluminum semi-weedless propeller**
● **Easy front filling gas tank**

Typically cheapest to obtain at vintage motor meets are what some buffs term "Eska types." From the 1960s through about 1985, the now-defunct bargain outboard maker Eska cranked out thousands upon thousands of lawnmower engine–powered kickers for itself and several dozen other labels. although not exotic, Eska-based motors can be serviced using parts from almost any small engine shop or home-and-garden center.

one: No matter how thoroughly you inspect the darn thing, at least one malady won't appear until *after* it's home. This fact of life accepted, be sure to check for common deal breakers that can be informally tested while pondering a purchase. (See Kicker Tip 1.3)

Also, ask whoever is offering the old outboard about its history. Pose questions like: Why are you selling it? What can you tell me about it? How well does it run? Responses containing proverbial used car salesman rhetoric should quickly send you on your way. A series of honest answers indicating the seller knows little about the motor is OK, providing the price reflects the risk you're being asked to take.

BEST BETS IN OLD OUTBOARDS BY DECADE

Even if a particular old outboard passes the tests outlined in Kicker Tip 1.3, it might be among those certain makes and models that are best avoided. Every hobby has its share of clunkers that those familiar with a particular pursuit learn to recognize and shun. Because bad news seems to travel faster and stay longer than positive feedback, devices reported to be problematic—although sometimes unfairly labeled—tend to get widespread scorn (a la the 1980s Yugo economy car).

On the other hand, certain makes and models of anything mechanical enjoy wide acceptance because they've

15

Kicker Tips 1.4
Official Outboard Honor Roll

These motors have earned reputations for sturdy construction, reliability, relative ease of repair, readily available parts, and respectable numbers still in use. Those marked in bold can be reasonably expected to show up for sale at Antique Outboard Motor Club meets, flea markets, and garage sales. One asterisk (*) indicates *acceptable*; two (**) are defined as *good*, and three (***) means *very good*.

Through 1919
Early magnetos were relatively weak, so battery ignition is preferred over flywheel magneto.
Caille rowboat motor **
Evinrude rowboat motor **
Lockwood rowboat motor **

1920s
Elto Ruddertwin (Has a rather complex ignition coil/timer system) *
Elto Speedster (Has a rather complex ignition coil/timer system) *
Johnson A and B series ***
Johnson opposed-cylinder K series ***

1930s
**Elto Ace, Handitwin, and Pal **
Evinrude Sportwin *
Evinrude/Elto Lightwin, Fisherman ***
**Evinrude Speeditwin #6039 (22.5-hp, through 1950) **
Johnson A-50 through A-80 *
Johnson model 100, 110, 200, 210 **
**Johnson PO series (22-hp, through 1950) **
**Neptune singles and twins *

1940s
**Elgin (West Bend-produced singles and non-shift twins. Sold by Sears.) **
**Evinrude Sportsman single (Switch-type fuel valve is typically problematic but can be repaired.) **
Gale Products (Buccaneer, Hiawatha, Royal, Sea-Bee, and Sea King, especially 1.5, 3, and 5-hp) *
**Johnson HD and TD **
**Johnson QD (10-hp with front-mounted shifter) *
**Martin 20, 40, and 60 **
Mercury Comet KE-3 single ***
Mercury Rocket KE-4 *
Mercury Lightning KE-7 **

Scott-Atwater 3.6-hp single (Also badge-engineered Firestone version) ***

1950s
Buccaneer and Gale singles and twins *
**Clinton air-cooled singles *
**Elgin (West Bend-produced) non-shift singles and twins **
Evinrude Lightwin *
**Evinrude Super Fastwin 15 and Fastwin 18 *
**Evinrude Big Twin 25 (Also 30- and 35-hp models) **
Johnson 3-hp JW *
**Johnson TN **
Johnson Sea Horse 5.5 **
Johnson QD (With side-mounted shift lever) **
Johnson Sea Horse 15 and 18 **
**Johnson RD **
**Martin (All make this Honor Roll except the rare 200. All but the 20, 60-CHS, and 200 can be commonly found.) **
**Mercury KF-5 Super Five (Beware of cracked lower-unit gearcase) *
Mercury KG-7 Hurricane **
Mercury Mark 20 and Mark 25 **
Scott-Atwater "Scotty" 3.6-hp single *
**Sea King (Gale Products–built) **
**Wizard (Mercury-built) **

1960s
**Chrysler singles and twins *
**Eska (Any model with air-cooled Tecumseh or Power Products single-cylinder engine. Also applies to various private-brand fishing motors with above powerhead types.) **
**Evinrude (Any two-cylinder except Lark with electric shift, or 9.5 Sportwin) **
Gale singles and twins **
**Johnson (Any two-cylinder except Electramatic Sea Horse 40 or Sea Horse 9.5) **
Mercury (Any single- or twin-cylinder except early-1960s automatic transmission models) **

1970s
Chrysler (See 1960s.)
Evinrude (All twin-cylinders except those with electric shift) **
**Evinrude Mate single (1.5-hp without rewind start is less troublesome than 2-hp version.) *
Force (Models under 20-hp) *
Johnson (All twins except electric shift) **
Johnson Sea Horse 1.5 single *
Mercury singles and twins ***

Early-1950s Mercury motors have enjoyed a long and devoted following in the classic-outboarding world. This 1952 Model KH-7 Cruiser was spotted in the Thousand Islands region of upstate New York. When revitalized by someone who knows what he or she is doing (and who has the proper tools), a Merc can be among the most enjoyably fast vintage outboards.

Typically, racing motors are more expensive and tougher to redo than their garden-variety sisters. The first day this pristine 1954 Mercury Mark 20H racer restoration was tried on a boat, bouncing waves caused the lower unit and prop to peek above the water. The motor revved way past redline specifications and blasted a connecting rod right through the crankcase!

Kicker Tips 1.5
She's a Must to Avoid

Evinrude
• **Zephyr.** A beautiful little 5.4-horsepower quad when properly maintained, but reputed to have a touchy ignition system and an overly complex carburetor.
• **Fleetwin.** With neutral clutch knob protruding from fuel tank. Troublesome shift mechanism.
• **Fastwin (14-horsepower).** Problems with early shifter, remote fuel tank system, and noisy powerhead.
• **Sportwin (alternate-firing).** Fuel gauge on front of tank. Prone to carb and fuel on/off switch problems.

Flambeau
Unconventional "sandwich" construction and proprietary carburetor

Johnson Model SD
Perhaps unfairly branded as the proverbial "clunker." Most of these 16-horsepower "tanks" appear to have much evidence of attempted repair.

Mercury
Late-1950s and early-1960s twins with automatic transmissions. Like *Alice in Wonderland*, "when they're good they're very, very good, but when they're bad they're horrid." Springs that control trannies can be difficult to deal with and require proprietary tools.

Scott (Scott-Atwater, and McCulloch)
Any model with "Bail-A-Matic." It's not necessarily the powerhead's fault, but the pump that is supposed to work the boat-bailing feature can malfunction to the detriment of the whole engine.

performed as advertised. To that better end, I give you *The Classic Outboard Motor Handbook*'s "Official Outboard Honor Roll" (See Kicker Tip 1.4). Admittedly, this listing represents the author's opinion, based on many fellow old-outboarders' observations and experiences. All motors included have earned reputations for sturdy construction, reliability, relative ease of repair, readily available parts, and respectable numbers still in use.

A FEW CAVEATS
In the mid-1960s, a pop song called "She's a Must to Avoid" hit the charts. Although this Herman's Hermits tune warned about falling for a beautiful but unreliably fickle young

With four cylinders and about 60 cubic iches of piston displacement, the Elto 4-60 can be a wonderful early-1930s project motor for those with a well-equipped shop and an appropriate boat. Finding such specialized racing outboards within most budgets, though, might represent an even bigger hurdle than bringing them back to life.

"Modern" motors such as these 1963 Evinrudes (left to right: 18-, 10-, 5-1/2-, and 3-horsepower) are good candidates for revitalization projects (unless horribly mistreated), because many replacement parts and service manuals can still be found. Many of these continue to provide reliable service, and those that currently don't can be picked up inexpensively from local marinas.

The author's son cradles the trusty 1947 Sea King Midget Single that he's had ever since he was barely big enough to rope-over the 1-horse eggbeater. Fact is, every buff usually cherishes his or her first classic motor, even if it doesn't always start.

A couple of true believers mug for the camera after returning from a defunct boat and motor shop with their third trailer load of vintage outboard parts. Hauls like this are decreasingly common now that most mom-and-pop marine establishments have given way to mega-retailers and Internet sales.

woman, it's used here to introduce a selected list of problematic motors and their related complaints (See Kicker Tip 1.5). None are too tough for an experienced outboard mechanic to tackle, but each has been the subject of enough swearing to warrant this cautionary advice. Some of these post-1940 outboards turn up at swap meets. Prior to their escape into the flea market world, they were probably doing time on some repair shop rack for at least two or three notorious reasons.

Regardless of which brand or model you choose from the good list, caution roster, or one that wasn't mentioned here, consider concentrating on one particular make, model, or year of manufacture. Your focus may then net you lots of specialized information about this favorite engine, rather than a smattering about a bunch of them. There's also a good chance you'll be in the loop to pick up some parts motors and parts that can be interchanged with other similar outboards in the collection.

CHAPTER 2

HOW AN OUTBOARD MOTOR WORKS

During the pioneering days of automobile travel, motorists were expected to possess a rich understanding of how every part on their horseless carriage functioned. Early car owners not blessed with such aptitude hired a mechanic to ride along. The same was true for folks with the first outboards. Nearly two decades after Evinrude's initial 1909 single-cylinder rowboat motor offering, the company's literature still stressed a do-it-yourself philosophy for its customers. "*There's a right way and wrong way . . .* that rule . . . applies to the care and maintenance of Evinrude Motors as it does to every other piece of machinery. Give your Evinrude the same consideration you'd give a watch [or auto]," the instruction manuals suggested, "and you'll find that [your outboard] is really built to last a decade!" Wouldn't the writer of that 1927 copy be surprised to see many of these vintage kickers still in operation?

The examples that do run nicely are typically owned by buffs who have acquired at least a basic understanding of small-engine operation and enjoy putting this knowledge to work on his or her particular classic outboard. Often, a great place to start is by memorizing a trio of conditions needed for any engine to run: **fuel**, **compression**, and **ignition**. Then, just like the mechanics from yesteryear—who always had those three conditions in mind—one can best visualize how a motor works by doing so in zones or systems, of which every outboard motor has five: **powerhead**, **ignition system, fuel system/carburetion**, **lower unit**, and **cooling system.** Admittedly, these gel into a clearer picture after a general overview of the two-cycle (interchangeably dubbed "two-stroke") engine, the type most prominent in all but a very few gas-fired old outboards.

THE MOST CLASSIC OUTBOARD ENGINE FORMAT

"The two-cycle outboard motor in many respects is more efficient than a four-cycle engine [as in one's car] of comparable piston displacement," 1950s powerboating pundit Hank Bowman was fond of noting. "Light weight per-horsepower-developed and a high horsepower-to-cubic inch-piston displacement are among the two-cycle's most favorable attributes," Bowman reminded.

That's why for decades, things that needed to be highly portable and high revving—like outboards, motorbikes, snowmobiles, chainsaws, compact lawn care power tools, and even model airplane engines—have successfully utilized two-stroke technology. Unlike an automotive or other four-cycle mill, in which the sparkplug fires every other time the engine's piston comes near the top of its cylinder, the two-stroke gets

A collector's arrangement of old iron, vintage oil cans, an engine shipping crate, and dealer signs makes for a museum-like motif in his basement. The kicker on the wooden stand is a nicely restored, late-1930s Elto Pal boasting just over a single horsepower. On calm water, it'd equal the effort of a good pair of oars.

A mid-1920s Johnson twin-cylinder (although only the left-hand cylinder is shown) powerhead in pieces. In addition to the cylinder, the bottom and top sections of the crankcase are shown, as are crankshaft, pistons on related connecting rods, and crankcase fasteners.

Kicker Tips 2.1

Before You Pull the Cord...

It's wise to know something about your newly acquired vintage outboard before trying it on the boat. The hour or so it'll take to go through the engine will be well worth the time. Here's a tried-and-true five-step plan developed by classic motor buff Art DeKalb, who has coaxed hundreds of once-defunct kickers back to life:

1. Clean out the gas tank, fuel lines, fuel valve, and filter.

2. Remove, disassemble, clean, and re-assemble the carburetor.

3. Pull the flywheel to gain access to the magneto. Check coil(s) and condenser, and then sand or file the points and set them for a proper opening gap. With the flywheel back on, check that the sparkplug works.

4. Check for healthy compression. Be sure the sparkplugs(s) are installed. If spinning the flywheel by hand, some "bounce back" is a good sign when the piston meets the resistance caused by compression. A compression gauge gives a more accurate picture.

5. Clean and check lower unit for leaking grease. A relentless ooze could mean bad seals, worn bushings, or maybe a crack in the lower unit/gearcase. Although it will push you over the "hour or so" labor-of-love estimate, decide to inspect the water pump (impeller, plunger, wobble agitator, or whatever type it possesses); look for clogging in the water intake or "telltale" outlet, if so equipped; and blow out any foreign matter from the water lines, if accessible. Pulling the gearcase cap (and propshaft) to inspect for water and rust is a good idea, too. Re-assemble, fill with lower-unit grease or oil. Inspect the propeller for damage that would call for filing out any major gouges or re-pitching its blades. Now you can mix some fuel (usually ½ pint of TCW-3 outboard oil to 1 gallon of gasoline), find a boat, and enjoy being mighty confident that the old gal will go!

an ignition flash to fire the compressed fuel/air mixture *each* time its piston reaches the apex. The blast causes the piston to race back down the cylinder and pick up more fuel for the next spark hit when it goes back up to repeat the routine. That means those busy-sounding little two-cycle powerplants sing such a tune because they're working twice the combustion impulses of their four-cycle sisters. Horsepower is generated with each set of down-and-up-again revolutions (or *two strokes*) of the powerhead's piston(s), connecting rod(s), and crankshaft. Two-cycle engines do this via simple fuel-intake and exhaust-cylinder ports and thus do not need the extra weight and complexity of horsepower-draining, mechanically operated valves-in-seats as found in four-stroke machinery. (Outboard history offers a couple exceptions to this pronouncement: 1946–1954 Martins and some late-1950s Oliver outboards were fitted with ingenious midwestern inventor George Martin's mechanically controlled *poppet* valves. These functioned as part of the carburetor manifold fuel intake, although not like the cylinder-incorporated valving on four-cycle engines.)

While on the topic of fuel, it should be noted that two-strokes have no crankcase oil reservoir, unlike four-cycle jobs. Instead, oil is mixed with the gasoline and gets dispersed through the engine's friction points. Two-cycle buffs like to point out that this is equivalent to treating one's engine to an automatic fresh oil change every time the motor is gassed up.

In order for the outboard powerhead's main internal components (piston, connecting rod, and crankshaft) to reciprocate at the operator's will, and consequently rotate the driveshaft, lower-unit gears, propeller shaft, and ultimately the propeller, each of the outboard motor's systems must function harmoniously. Similar to what future doctors are taught during medical training, it must be pointed out that specialization best begins with a useful generalized understanding of each motor part in the distinct systems and their possible relationships (healthy and harmful) to one another.

THE POWERHEAD

If outboard motors could bow their powerheads and pray, they'd probably ask the Good Lord to protect them from every engine's biggest enemy: excessive friction. This stress is a byproduct of the powerhead's necessary internal motion involving the following parts:

• **Crankcase** encases the crankshaft, houses the reed valves (if applicable), and hosts the carburetor.

• **Crankshaft** has "steps" or "throws" that allow the pistons (which are connected to the crankshaft via connecting rods) to travel back and forth within the cylinder(s).

• **Connecting rod** serves as a moving bridge between the crankshaft and piston.

• **Endcap** of the connecting rod secures the large end of the connecting rod to the crankshaft while grasping the piston via the wristpin.

Factory-produced Johnson promotional cutaways like this offered enthusiasts a look inside at the flywheel and fuel tank.

The same Johnson Sea Horse 5 cutaway reveals portions of the crankshaft and pistons in their cylinders. The electric motor visible at the front drives this display piece, while red bulbs in the cylinder head flash to simulate spark.

• **Wristpin** mates piston to connecting rod and allows both to move sideways a bit.

• **Piston** travels in the cylinder and rushes toward the sparkplug, having just been influenced by crankcase pressure from the induction of fresh fuel/air mixture through the crankcase and into the cylinder. It's pushed down again by the ignition explosion, repeating the process.

• **Piston rings** expand outward from their groove in the outer diameter of the piston *seating* and endeavor to create a tighter piston seal (and thus better compression) than would be the case without these relatively springy bands.

• **Cylinder** hosts the piston and contains ports needed for fuel/air intake and exhaust. Sometimes the cylinder is cast in one piece with the crankcase.

• **Flywheel** provides balance and inertia for the crankshaft motion, and provides a useful place to rotate the major powerhead components for starting.

• **Reed valves** serve as miniature gatekeepers between the carburetor and crankcase to let fresh fuel mixture in, but not out on the upstroke.

• **Exhaust assemblies,** in the form of external mufflers, are primarily found on pre–World War II models. These usually consist of "cans" attached to a manifold that's connected to the cylinder or cylinders. Newer models send exhaust down an exhaust tube or into the motor leg.

Crucial to reducing friction wherever there is metal-against-metal motion are the powerhead's bearings. They are like little beds in which parts, such as the crankshaft as

Connecting rod and endcap. Note the bronze bearings inlaid in the endcap to "bush" the piston's wristpin and the crankshaft "throw." Sharp-eyed readers will also catch the tiny sheet metal tab washers under the endcap bolt heads. These are pushed against the tightened bolt to keep it from wiggling loose.

The reed valve on its reed plate serves to properly deliver the fuel/air mixture from the carburetor to the crankcase and on to the combustion chamber. Needless to say, the reeds must be positioned within a factory-specified tolerance. On most motors that haven't been tampered with, though, they're OK.

21

A simple magneto for a single-cylinder outboard. The magnet (center disc) rotates on the crankshaft around the heel and coil. The points (right-hand side) open and close in time with a cam. The condenser (partially obscured by points mechanism) is one of the "mag's" other vital components and in a long-unused kicker typically needs replacing.

Many 1950s coils were dipped into a protective plastic coating that cracks with age. This mag plate (minus its points and condensers) shows that both coils have shed their cracked plastic shells and, as a result, need replacement. As a general rule, alternate-firing engines have one coil (and point set) per cylinder, while opposed-cylinder motors wear one coil and point set per bank of cylinders.

it fits into the crankcase/cylinder assembly, ride "cushioned" from pressures that (in the case of an outboard motor) would otherwise be associated with a hardened steel crankshaft rotating in an aluminum crankcase. If eventually worn out, bearings can be replaced. Bearings are usually classified in two types:

1. Friction bearings (also dubbed "plain bearings" or "bushings") are predominantly of bronze construction.

2. Non-friction bearings (sometimes called "jeweled," "ball," "needle," or "roller" bearings) have rolling surfaces that share friction points in such a way that makes the work easier. Imagine this type as a group of cut off broom handles or marbles placed between a heavy box and a concrete floor. Motion to that box would occur much more easily (because of reduced friction) than if a piece of cardboard were used as a bearing between those two surfaces.

In practice, both bearing names are euphemistic, as even the non-friction type is subject to some friction, and the friction-style certainly offers less friction than if it were not employed at all in the friction point. No matter, power-head bearings and the parts they comfort must be within proper tolerances (as suggested by the motor maker) or moving parts will be too loose (causing knocking) or too tight (promoting possible engine seizure and metal warpage or breakage).

THE IGNITION SYSTEM

Although some early outboards, including the fun-to-operate 1920s and early-1930s Elto Ruddertwin and Speedster, got spark from a battery, coil, condenser, and timer, most old kickers likely to be encountered today use a magneto ignition. A magneto assembly is actually a small generator whose sole purpose is providing electricity to the

sparkplug(s) at the precise time that the plug is supposed to fire the cylinder's compressed fuel/air mixture. The magneto assembly typically sits on a plate located under the flywheel. This *stator* or *mag plate* has a hole in its center to allow for the protrusion of the top of the crankshaft. When the magnets in the flywheel (or sometimes a disc magnet that's located just under the flywheel and keyed to the crankshaft) rotate around a metal *heel* attached to an ignition coil, electrical current is built up and surges through the coil's primary (thin copper wire) windings.

A 1930s Evinrude/Elto-style poppet-valve carburetor with its float bowl cover removed lies on its side. The needle valve adjustment lever and fuel line connector (visible behind the float bowl) are also evident. The poppet valve and its related spring is behind the other three-screw cover. Wire is wrapped around the screws to keep them in place while the carb is off the motor.

OMC pressurized, two-hose remote fuel tanks like this were used with motors dating from 1949 through the late 1950s. A lot can go wrong with one that didn't receive proper care and storage. If negotiating for an Evinrude or Johnson that uses a pressure tank, make sure that the deal includes a working example.

Some 1950s Mercury products also utilized a pressurized, double-hose remote fuel tank system. This one, which came with a Merc-built Western Auto Wizard outboard, is missing the hose and its even tougher-to-find fuel-to-engine fitting. A trigger opens the section of handle that reveals the tank lid. If the originally flexible rubber gasket boot in the tank's mouth becomes hardened, sufficient pressure won't build. Watch out for pinched fingers when clicking these tank lids closed!

Next, magnetic energy pulls the juice into the magneto's secondary coil windings and through the sparkplug wire (or high-tension lead) to the plug and its spark-jump gap. A condenser helps keep the voltage strong by momentarily storing power from the primary windings and zapping it into the secondary just in time to ride along to the spark-plug with the secondary's other juice. The spark is properly timed by a set of points that signal the circuit to release electricity to the plug. These *breaker* points open and close at the command of a rotating cam on the crankshaft. The stator's position in relationship to the cam's *bump* can either advance or retard this timing. That's one reason the motor can be slowed or sped up by moving the lever attached to the stator.

THE FUEL/CARBURETION SYSTEM
On the most basic old, two-stroke outboards, the gas/oil mixture is gravity fed to the carburetor from an integral (to the motor) tank via a filter (screen), shut-off valve, elbows, and fuel line. Along the way, the line can get clogged with anything from aged gas to pine needles. The object is to ensure the carburetor a generous supply of clean fuel. Once there, it receives the carburetor's primary service of mixing (or metering) the gas/oil mixture with air and then sending the brew into the crankcase and onto the cylinder's combustion chamber. The carburetor typically has several components:
- **The carburetor body,** which comprises a fuel bowl, air and fuel passages, and needle valve seats.
- **The float and pin valve.** When a sufficient fuel supply is in the fuel bowl, the (cork or brass) float rises, and its associated pin (with a check valve at the bottom end) suspends fuel flow from the tank.

Single-hose tanks like this West Bend–built Sears' Elgin remote fuel "Reservoir" can most typically be cleaned and reused. No pressure is needed in the tank to push fuel to the engine. While this private brand Elgin example is an uncommon find, it is minus its hose, squeeze bulb, and connector. These can be replaced with parts stocked in Wal-Mart, but that ring of rust around the tank's base might signal crud in the bottom that would cause most buffs to get a modern plastic replacement tank while they're shopping for the aforementioned stuff.

- **The butterfly valve** or throttle acts as a little hand in the carb body to increase or slow the fuel/air mixture flow to the crankcase.
- **The choke** can cut off the air supply when a primarily gas/oil (termed "rich") mixture will help with cold starting.
- **Needle valves** are used to ensure optimum fuel flow to jets in the carburetor body.
- **A fuel filter** is made from screen or a porous element within a glass filter bowl assembly.
- **Gaskets** keep the fuel/air mix in and dirt out.

Classic outboards with remote gas tanks pull their fuel

The bronze tube to the left of this gearcase cap (through which the propeller shaft runs) will serve as a prop shaft bushing as soon as it is tightly fitted into the aluminum piece. The bushing provides a less-wearing surface for the stainless steel propeller shaft than would bare aluminum.

to the carburetor either by a two-hose (fuel and air) **pressurized system,** whereby air pressure builds up in a non-vented tank, or via a single-hose (with primer bulb) **non-pressurized system** employing a vented tank and crankcase-mounted fuel pump that typically operates with vacuum air pulses created by crankcase compression. The pressurized version was popular from the late 1940s through much of the 1950s, but its relatively complex fuel tanks required decompression by loosening the tank cap after each outing. Mariners were glad to see this method go the way of the wind, or "whoosh," as the air pressure escape sighed.

THE LOWER UNIT

"Out of sight, out of mind, and out of luck" is one vintage outboarder's mantra about the pitfalls of neglecting a kicker's lower unit. After all, if the system that includes an outboard's means of propulsion doesn't function well, the rest of the motor is moot. Worthy of note are:

• **The gearcase,** which houses the works (gears, bearings, and seals).

• **The skeg** aids in steering and protects the propeller.

• **The gears** transfer power from the driveshaft to the propshaft and in shift models facilitate neutral and reverse, as well as forward. Shifting occurs when a *dog clutch* mechanism moves propshaft-mounted gears into the desired position.

• **The lower-unit seals** keep grease in the gearcase and water away from internal components.

• **The lower-unit bearings** reduce friction points.

• **The driveshaft** takes power from the crankshaft and delivers it to the propshaft.

• **The propshaft** is driven through gears in almost all outboards, and it rotates the propeller.

• **The propeller** is described by the diameter and pitch its blades use to push a boat through water.

THE COOLING SYSTEM

The vast majority of outboards from any era are cooled by water that's pumped from the lake, river, pond, or ocean, circulated through the powerhead's cylinder area, and then returned to nature. Most kickers also use some of this water to cool off and muffle exhaust passages. "Water jackets," or passageways cast inside the cylinder, allow water to circulate just a fraction of an inch from where combustion takes place. On running motors with exposed cylinders, the operator should be able to touch the jacketed zone of the cylinder without it feeling like a hot stove. In fact, many buffs include tapping a finger on the cylinder(s) and checking to be sure that cooling water is squirting through their kicker's "telltale" exit opening (if so equipped) as part of the starting routine.

The older and less sophisticated the outboard, the more likely it'll use a series of external tubes and fittings to convey the water. This piping and the related water intake need to be free of obstructions.

A *positive-type* water pump, typical of most water-cooled motors, works when its starfish-like impeller whirls in the pump body. Other pumps operate with either a plunger (activated by a cam) or wobbling agitator method. Antiques including the Elto Speedster and Johnson A-35 employ a *water scoop* or siphoning action that transmits cooling water without a mechanical pump. The faster the boat traveled, the better the water circulated. As a result, anglers using these old models for trolling sometimes cooked their cylinders.

Looking for signs that one's classic kicker is cooling is an extremely simple but crucial step every buff can instantly master. Even the most modern mariner with a brand-new outboard is expected by the manufacturer to know about the importance of ensuring that the motor is pumping that vital cooling water.

An outboard motor cylinder with its cylinder head removed shows the water jacket passageways between the head studs. On some saltwater motors or engines long neglected, these channels can be filled solid with rust, scale, salt, or mud from insects. Patient poking, picking, and subjection to compressed air can offer a cure.

CHAPTER 3
EQUIPPING A HOME-BASED OUTBOARD REPAIR SHOP

Sometime during the first weeks of the 1958 boating season, a pulpy, 75-cent "how-to" magazine featured an article called "Handymen, You Can Make Money Servicing Outboard Motors." The editors of that edition of *Boat Builder's Handbook* figured they'd hit upon a topic capable of attracting readers who were thinking about cashing in on the most ubiquitous sideline to result from the 1950s boating boom: maintaining some of the five million outboards then in use. Central to such a venture, suggested writer Bob Whittier, was establishing an efficient place in one's garage or basement to conduct these potentially profitable repairs.

While *The Classic Outboard Motor Handbook* is intended for hobbyists, rather than Eisenhower-era entrepreneurs, the 1958 motor servicing article began with a word of caution that I wish I'd read prior my first home-based setup. Whittier warned that even a little leftover gas/oil mixture "dripping from [an outboard's] carburetor and fuel line couplings will fill the house with gasoline odor." Once, as a teenager and proud new owner of a very worn out brand-X kicker, I enthusiastically started its revitalization in my bedroom. Of course, the newspaper I'd put under the motor stand to catch dirt and stuff only made things worse when soaking up about a half pint of antique fuel that came with the decrepit engine. For days, the entire upstairs smelled like a poorly managed gas station. Needless to say, my parents were none too happy, nor were they appeased when I quickly toted the outboard to the basement, inadvertently dribbling fuel along the way. Even the tiny basement alcove I commandeered for a motor fixit shop began wafting gasoline fumes.

After listening to my mother fret about how the gas could cause our house to explode, my dad wisely devised a two-step plan, whereby all wayward outboards were fully drained, cleaned, and aired-out prior to being racked in the basement. There's no trick to draining the fuel other than recognizing that even after the main fuel tank is emptied, small quantities of gas/oil will likely hide there as well as in

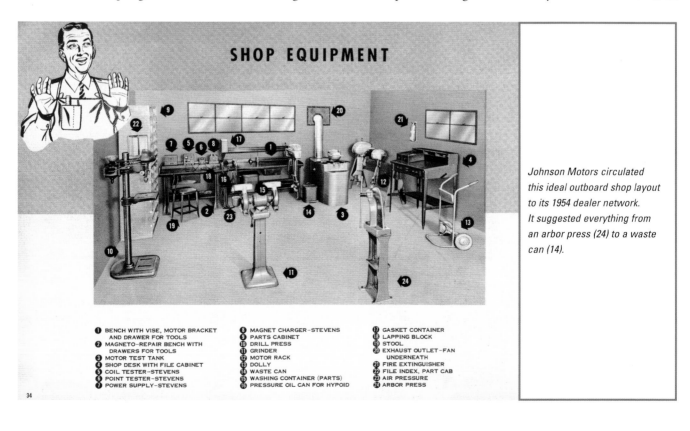

SHOP EQUIPMENT

1. BENCH WITH VISE, MOTOR BRACKET AND DRAWER FOR TOOLS
2. MAGNETO-REPAIR BENCH WITH DRAWERS FOR TOOLS
3. MOTOR TEST TANK
4. SHOP DESK WITH FILE CABINET
5. COIL TESTER–STEVENS
6. POINT TESTER–STEVENS
7. POWER SUPPLY–STEVENS
8. MAGNET CHARGER–STEVENS
9. PARTS CABINET
10. DRILL PRESS
11. GRINDER
12. MOTOR RACK
13. DOLLY
14. WASTE CAN
15. WASHING CONTAINER (PARTS)
16. PRESSURE OIL CAN FOR HYPOID
17. GASKET CONTAINER
18. LAPPING BLOCK
19. STOOL
20. EXHAUST OUTLET–FAN UNDERNEATH
21. FIRE EXTINGUISHER
22. FILE INDEX, PART CAB
23. AIR PRESSURE
24. ARBOR PRESS

Johnson Motors circulated this ideal outboard shop layout to its 1954 dealer network. It suggested everything from an arbor press (24) to a waste can (14).

34

The main shop area where a majority of The Classic Outboard Motor Handbook*'s test cases got their TLC. Notice the small and low (2-1/2x4-foot) workbench holding a large vise, a wire brush on an electric motor, and a bench grinder. Space saved is used for parts drawers, while a shelf underneath the bench is reserved for a stack of shop rags and tools. The bench is also home to two flexible-neck lamps. The block of wood leaning against the left side of the bench is ready to be put into the vise and used as a motor stand. The modest bench width allows the mechanic to easily access wall-mounted tools on the pegboard.*

the fuel line and carb bowl. So, persistence and a few days of letting the motor dry out in a nonliving area are in order.

In that condition, a motor is better suited for operation in any space attached to the house. Suffice it to say, even several ounces of gas and oil—especially if it has been sitting in the tank or carb for a while—can upset one's family members. Key to enjoying the pursuit of restoring classic outboards is ensuring that those close to you are happy that you have an interesting and nontoxic hobby.

FROM THE FLOOR UP

There's an old-outboard buff who likes to tell me about his shop floor. He bought one of those 8x16-foot garden shed kits, and because the local concrete company wouldn't risk trucking cement across his soggy yard, built the little structure on 4x4-inch posts and gave it a ¾-inch plywood floor. The guy loves to explain how, because of the wood and a nice airspace between floor and ground, his motors don't rust while stored in the shed.

There is a lot to be said for a wooden floor, especially after standing on it for a few hours. Wood can be warmer and easier on the feet than concrete. And when installed with a vapor barrier, wood tends to cut down on rusting that's inevitable when moisture seeps through concrete. That's not to dismiss the typical cement basement or garage floor, but even a 4x8-foot or 8x8-foot riser section of plywood on a sturdy frame of 2x4s makes a nice spot for motor work. No matter what kind of shop flooring you choose, it can be greatly improved for outboard repairs via

a coat of light-color paint. I've seen one home shop with a shade of yellow reminiscent of those happy-face Wal-Mart characters. Although sometimes seemingly a bit too cheery, such a hue often makes finding the inevitably dropped parts much easier. If you're starting from scratch, as opposed to using leftover paint from some kitchen-remodeling project, light gray is considered *the* standard shop-floor color. Wooden or cement, these surfaces should be thoroughly cleaned and smoothed over before painting. That is to say, any crack or gap eager to swallow up small screws, nuts, bolts, washers, springs, or other hardware should be filled with an appropriate-use compound. My experience has led me to believe that every outboard revitalization session contains at least one major search for a tiny something that "*has* to be around here somewhere!" Smooth, light-color shop floors, free of crevices and obstructions make restoration much more fun. Being able to quickly note, "Oh there it is, easily detected on my nice, light-colored floor" brings untold satisfaction.

CAN'T SEE A DARN THING!

Imagine entering a doctor's examining room and discovering it's lit with a single 75-watt bulb hanging from the ceiling. Then, picture your physician complaining that he just can't make a proper diagnosis because the light is so bad. Now, think how a vintage outboard might feel being examined by a home mechanic in a poorly illuminated shop. If we can consider light to be a useful tool, there's ample justification to include adequate wiring and lighting

This view from the corner of the author's shop shows a portion of the waste-high, 4x8-foot workbench positioned for three-sided access. This means that tools are at the mechanic's back, but parts can be attacked from multiple areas of the bench. An old dresser (visible under the left-hand side of the white pegboard) provides drawers for storage and a flat surface for boxed tools.

fixtures in the shop preparation budget. Of course, in nice weather one can work outside in the sunshine. Just don't drop any small motor parts near a hungry squirrel.

While traditional white porcelain "bare bulb/pull string" sockets (probably already in your place) can provide backup, they're best used as junction boxes in which new outlets for better lighting can be wired. And, fluorescent is really the way to go. Today's low-watt units (such as fixtures with a pair of 4-foot, 32-watt fluorescent tubes) are economically priced and perform much better than their flickering, slow starting, and buzzing ancestors. Ideally, these shop lights should be positioned over the workbench and above the spot where you'll be fixing the motor. Considering that the brightness emitted by $50 to $100 worth of fluorescent fixtures and related wiring can actually lift one's spirits, it's amazing more shops don't bother with such a vital detail. For those not comfortable with installing a few extra outlet boxes, much improved lighting is even worth the cost of an hour or two of an electrician's time.

By the way, ample receptacles should be made available for plugging in power tools and a radio. The rule of thumb is to figure out how many things you'll have plugged in at once and then double that number to determine how many outlets you'll need. Avoiding multiple extension cords and those plastic outlet extender adaptors is always prudent.

APPROACHING THE BENCH

The Johnson Motor Company recommended that each of its dealers have at least one workbench, 2 to 2-1/2 feet wide and 6 to 8 feet long. That famous outboard maker's 1956 service planning booklet stated: "Work benches can be made to fit [your shop's] individual floor plan. They must, however, be of rugged construction to withstand hard use. Benches made entirely of wood are satisfactory, but metal bench [framework] will really stand up to all kinds of work conditions. Bench tops can be laid with 2x6 or 2x8-inch planks securely fastened to together and to the [metal] bench frame standards."

Johnson was always big on workbenches having a couple of drawers for tools and supplies. A medium-size or large vise also made the manufacturer's must-have list. Equally important for its Sea Horse service centers was a minimum of "one motor bracket attached to each bench. This provides a simple and convenient method of working on the motor in that it is placed on the mechanic's bench, near to tools."

The previously mentioned "Handymen" article figured 3x8 feet is a good outboard workbench dimension. This "bench must be rigid. Its top should have no cracks through which tiny parts could fall, and it should have a retaining molding around its edge. A 2x8-inch plank [can be attached] to the bench in a vertical position to hold the powerhead of most outboard motors at about chest level." While I wholeheartedly concur with Johnson and Whittier about workbench sturdiness, my favorite was built with a 4x8-foot sheet of 3/4-inch plywood on a 2x6-inch pine frame. Not a single nail went into the project, as the framework was bolted together and Sheetrock screws were affixed the top. On this generous surface, one can lay out a host of

Kicker Tips 3.1
A Long List of Shop Shortcuts

1. Arrange screwdrivers and wrenches in graduated sizes, with the smallest to the left.
2. Return tools to their pegs (cabinet or holder) right after you finish using them. Things are much easier to find again when they're in their usual place.
3. Avoid doubling up tools on a single peg.
4. Dust the workbench and sweep the shop floor whenever there's a big enough pile of debris in which small screws and parts can hide.
5. Always have some paper towels handy and in a secure holder so you can tear off a length of them with one hand.
6. Arrange small squirt cans of machine and penetrating oil in a readily accessible place that does not wobble when the workbench or pegboard is touched.
7. Keep shop oils and solvents away from kids, pets, and electrical outlets.
8. Check the local kitchen-remodeling store for old cabinets that they removed on a job. These make great storage areas for all kinds of tools, parts, and test equipment.
9. When wire-brushing, sanding, or polishing, be sure to wear eye protection and a facemask. Some like to don a lightweight welder's face shield that allows one to also wear regular eyeglasses.
10. Always have a clean and safe spot in your shop to set down a cup of coffee, a soft drink, or a donut!

Install as much pegboard as possible in your workshop. This space has some on every wall, with this corner reserved for pegged jar tops and plastic baby food jar–type containers offering a quick view of available nuts, bolts, etc. Note, too, the handy paper-towel holder (lower right) and the test-wheel propeller substitutes hanging on nails to the right.

Don't disregard useful and decorative shop accessories, even if they don't have an overt boating theme. One outboard collector found several of these sparkplug advertising-emblazoned parts holders at a vintage-car flea market.

tools and parts for the job. Plus, there's ample space for a clipboard, scrap paper, and a service manual. For workbenches wider than about 3 feet, position them away from walls with easy access all the way around.

When planning your bench, consider its proposed height and whether you'll typically stand or sit while working. Finally, no matter how you approach your bench, even a little wiggle can be annoying. That's why bolts (as opposed to nails) are so important. Most home centers sell metal bracing brackets for making workbenches rock solid.

GET YOUR TOOLS PEGGED

There's a goofy tale about a 1920s mob hit on a back-alley Chicago auto repair shop that was actually a front for some rival crime boss. No one got rubbed out that day, but soon after the gunfire stopped and the getaway car screeched out of sight, a mechanic got the idea to place strategically bent coat hanger wire into the dozens of bullet holes above his workbench. You guessed it! On those wire hooks, he arranged his tools and the idea for pegboard was born.

Although surely not historically accurate, the story reminds shop planners that, like a mobster considering how many bodyguards to employ in a gang war, there is no such thing as too many hooks or too much pegboard space. A full 4x8-foot sheet of the useful surface should be considered minimum. Most home centers and lumber stores offer pegboard in a few different thicknesses and colors. (The sheets with the most substantial dimension are usually worth the extra dollar or two.)

White is best for highlighting tools and brightening up the shop a bit. Somewhere along pegboard's development chronology, the hole sizes were increased slightly. Make sure the pegs and accessories you want will easily fit into the board's holes. I bought a small riverside house that came with a couple of pegboard sections in the workshop. After struggling with the installation of "modern" sized hooks and screwdriver racks (and having to drill out some holes), I purchased a couple of sheets of the new stuff and never looked back. If your workbench is along a wall, tradition calls for pegboard to be securely mounted to that wall, giving quick tool access. Most folks who've affixed their pegboard to scrap lumber nailed upward on the bench eventually get sufficiently aggravated by rattling or falling tools whenever the bench is jiggled. It's best to mount the pegboard independent of the workbench. In my basement shop, where the bench sits in the middle of the room, I ran a pair of 8-foot, 2x3-inch "economy studs" from the ceiling joists to the basement floor. I then hung a sheet of pegboard on each 3-inch face of the studs to double my pegboard space. On one side, I have mechanic's tools and plastic peg jars filled with nuts, bolts, and screws, while the other board is reserved for woodworking gear. One shop I visited used this method (two pegboard "walls" in an L-shaped arrangement) to neatly divide the work area from an informal family room.

Finally, some buffs swear there's great wisdom in finishing off one's pegboard project by outlining (with a permanent marker) each tool that's pegged. That way, it's easy to see where tools should be returned when not in use.

MOTORS IN GOOD STANDING

Like many outboarders, my first motor stand was nothing more than an old, wobbly sawhorse. It was rather loosely held together with nails in constant need of re-pounding, and it had so many wounds from careless saw teeth that the pathetic thing eventually collapsed. That crash provided a painful lesson, because the paint-splattered sawhorse was at the time home to one of my most prized vintage outboards. While tearfully surveying the motor's newly dented fuel tank, I vowed to invest in some substantial stands.

From the earliest days of outboarding, motor makers and aftermarket accessory firms have offered single-engine-sized stands. One of the most popular is typically called the "OMC tube-type." For some 40 years, these postwar, lightweight stands were used in Johnson and Evinrude showrooms (until OMC began displaying new motors in the bottom portions of their shipping cartons), as well as a staple in the old Outboard Marine Corporation's consumer accessory catalogs. Thousands are still in existence and can sometimes be purchased used from marine dealers or outboard collectors.

Two basic sizes were made: one for motors up to 40 horses, and a heftier one for bigger engines. Either denomination makes for a good main work stand. Collectors with more than about 10 outboards, however, claim that multiple OMC stands take up too much space to be used exclusively. For storing a lot of kickers, enthusiasts go with their own custom-built wooden stands. Advice from these buffs is universal: Construct whatever suits your needs, but be sure that the unit is made with substantial lumber that's bolted (not nailed) together. Depending on what size outboards you have, the stand's motor boards can be anything from 2x6 to 2x12-inch planks. While similar sizing is acceptable for the legs and, if desired, base, 4x4 lumber always answers the call for ruggedness. I've had

Vintage outboard–related dealer signage like this eye-catching electric octagon really dress up a shop, but are often quite expensive. Reproduction signs and clocks add pretty much the same visual intrigue at a fraction of antique costs.

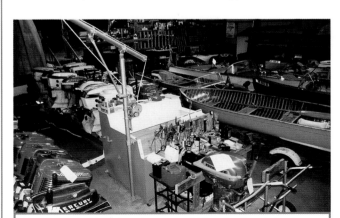

The blue and white unit at the center of this collection of classic motors and boats is a test tank with an attached tool rack and nearby workbench. A boom and winch are used to hoist big motors into the drink so they can be fine-tuned.

A double row of motors with their lower units bagged. This collector didn't want any gearcase oil drips on his floor, so he stuck paper towels on the skegs and then held the toweling in place with plastic shopping bags. Some buffs fold a square of paper towel onto the skeg and then secure it with a clothespin. Others use potpie trays.

Up-and-down motor storage via a 2x8-inch rail attached to appropriately thick spacers on wall studs. The spacers are needed to give the motors needed clearance from the shop wall. A 33.4-horsepower Evinrude SpeediFour rests comfortably on a large OMC tube stand.

success with a simple design of two 4x4s vertically mounted (10 feet apart) from ceiling joists to basement floor, with an upper (10 foot) length of 2x6 plank for small outboards, and a lower level run of 2x8 pine for the heavier engines. Others have good luck with freestanding, single-tier stands built like heavy-duty sawhorses. Stands on substantial casters or wheels also come in handy. An extremely useful gadget for any outboard fan is an aftermarket single-motor stand on wheels. I look for reasonably priced (under $30) examples whenever perusing flea markets or garage sales.

In the workbench section, I mentioned the value of bench-mounted work stands. Just be sure it won't tip the bench over when it's holding a hefty engine. One of my Antique Outboard Motor Club compatriots has restored scores of motors secured to a 2-foot piece of 2x6-inch oak tightened in the bench vise. If you go this ingeniously simple route, be sure that the vise has adequate grip and that you won't need to use it for anything else. I've seen a restorer forced to heft a bulky motor off this sort of stand several times when a more traditional use for the vise suddenly arose. A key to enjoyable shop use is the avoidance of having to take two steps backward in order to gain one pace forward. Then again, there is something to be said for simplicity. It all depends on where you *stand* (pun intended) on this important outboard storage issue.

THIS IS ONLY A TEST!

Forgive my references to my childhood outboard revitalization experiences, but many of those novice days forced me to learn good lessons that may be helpful to others in the hobby. Two tales come to mind. The first involves starting a 9/10-horsepower 1937 Evinrude Scout in my bedroom in a sheet metal wastepaper basket filled with bathtub water. That was just plain dumb over-enthusiasm that cost me several weeks of anticipated TV viewing and a good chunk of my allowance for repairs to the living room ceiling. Then there was the "ruined good clothes/shoes incident." Although it involved a legitimate 55-gallon oil drum, surprising turbulence from the prop and water action in that greasy, smoky barrel quickly gushed goopy liquid all over the immediate vicinity of my Sunday-morning motor test. I suppose the fact that this was only about two minutes before the family was heading off to church made things worse.

Professional shops often have commercially built outboard test tanks that are far superior to either the wastebasket or oil drum styles. A favorite tank of the 1950s came from Stolper Steel Products (Menomonee, Wisconsin) with a 50x29-inch outer diameter. Its oval shape and rear splashguard allowed prop wash to circulate without spilling all over the floor. Some pro tanks even feature exhaust stacks and fans that allow a measure of indoor use. Like the aforementioned commercial motor stands, these tanks occasionally become available from collectors and downsized marine establishments.

Although this 1953 Johnson model TN Sea Horse 5 cutaway revealing its internal powerhead and water pump is interesting, for our purposes the real focal point of this shot is the standard-size (up to 40-horsepower) OMC tube stand on which the motor sits. Lightweight and sturdy, these useful stands can be quickly dismantled by pulling the tubular legs out of the stand head. Every home outboard shop would be well served with at least one. They're also perfect for toting to vintage boat shows. Over the years there were several slightly different heads on these units (in addition to an altogether larger stand), and not every one will accommodate all motors up to 40 horses.

This wooden test tank is internally caulked and painted to make it watertight. When its lid is closed, the tank simply appears to be a potting stand in keeping with the gardening décor of its surroundings. The little Evinrude is kicking up suds because the shop master religiously squirts a bit of dishwashing liquid into the tank prior to use. That way, there's no oily residue on the lower unit when the outboard is removed.

For those competent in carpentry, a rectangular test tank made with wood and coated inside with sheet metal or made watertight via caulking or some other method is also a way to go. One outboarder built one such tank next to a similarly sized box (used for garden compost) right outside his garage/workshop. Covered with hatch doors, both look pleasingly benign in the side yard. Being able to test your latest motor project in conditions mimicking boat operation makes test tanks incredibly valuable tools. By the way, some motors (such as the Mercury 39 in Chapter 5) are fitted with a threaded port to which a garden-hose flushing attachment can be installed. Typically, though, the modern outboard hose flushers of the earmuff-type aren't compatible with water intakes on vintage motors.

THE TOOL LIST

Somewhere on my shop pegboard there's a small, cheap, poorly aligned, rough, sand-cast pair of pliers. They are all that remains of a child-size tool kit my dad bought me when I was in kindergarten. Every once in a while, I'll use them to do some easy job like pull a cotter pin from a propeller shaft. Other than that, they're not much good. Still, I'd never consider parting with those pliers. Such is the power of sentiment when it comes to otherwise junky inanimate objects like certain workshop tools. They can become like old friends—quirky but loyal. It is in this spirit that I recommend gathering a group of tools typically helpful during most outboard restoration adventures.

Although a generalization, most mechanics agree that American tools are worth the extra money over imported items. Because of the often significantly lower price of imports from the Far East, though, one of my fellow outboarders has a shop largely equipped with Chinese-made tools. While economy in selection makes a certain degree of sense, it leads me to suggest staying within budget by cruising flea markets and estate auctions for quality U.S.-made tools at reasonable prices. As a historical bonus, many of these will be from the 1940s and 1950s, just like some classic outboards. In front of an old house one summer Friday afternoon, I found a tag sale featuring among the boxes of books, record albums, and clothes, a 5-gallon kitty litter pail filled with a slightly rusty windfall tangle of classic Craftsman, Millers Falls, Stanley, Proto, and other high-grade American tools. Price, 10 bucks! It likely represented someone's careful lifetime amassing of quality implements. They shined up pretty nicely, too.

If a stubborn nut, bolt, or screw has a useable head, an impact driver can be used to break it free.

A simple way to test whether or not your outboard's magneto produces fire under compression, Ignition Chek can also quickly identify bad coils that would otherwise look fine when the spark is tested in the open air.

For many collectors, the chase is much of the fun. No one says a shop must be instantly stocked. Basic things, like a few popular-size wrenches and screwdrivers, need to be available from the start, but much of the remaining gear on the following list may be had in a long series of acquisitions that one may savor:

Screwdrivers. As long as they're high-quality, nicely hardened alloy, go wild here. Pick ones with a pleasant-to-handle grip in your favorite translucent colors, in standard slot and Phillips head. All sizes will come in handy. Be sure at least one bigger screwdriver (in each type) has a square shaft so that an adjustable wrench can be applied for extra turning force. A flexible shaft version and an offset type will also come in handy.

Adjustable wrenches. An 8-incher will likely become one of your most used tools. As a high school junior working at a donut shop, I bought an 8-inch Snap-on brand adjustable from a jobber who stopped in for coffee. It's played a role in each of my motor projects, and even managed to survive a couple of inadvertent trips through the washing machine when left in a jacket pocket. Incidentally, 10- and 12-inch versions are nice to have, too.

Open-end wrenches. Get them one at a time or in a set ranging from 5/16 to 3/4 inch. Add other denominations as desired.

Box wrenches. Even though they do the same thing as their open-ended (or fork-type) brethren, box wrenches can provide a surer grasp on a stubborn nut or bolt head.

Socket wrenches and related accessories. To amass a good range of standard length and deep sockets in 1/4-, 3/8-, and 1/2-inch denominations, one could spend a lifetime. And then there are all of the possibilities in extenders, swivels, and 1/2-to-3/8-inch reducers! It's OK to begin with a compromise and get a good 3/8-inch drive starter set and add more as needed. Make sure they're not metric sizes unless you want to work on vintage foreign outboards.

Hex wrenches. Fancy ones with plastic coated handles are nice, but the little L-shaped sets or the kind that fold out like pocketknife blades work, too.

Hammers and mallets. In addition to the standard carpenter hammer, don't forget a small ballpeen and wooden-, plastic-, or rubber-head mallets. Some old motor revitalization projects require a surprising number of bangs and tapping.

Pliers. Standard, locking (Vise-Grips), long-nose, and pliers with crevices in the grab area are all helpful in engine projects. The latter are used when dealing with flexible wire clamps often found on rubber fuel hoses.

Feeler gauge. While neither big nor expensive, this tool is worth 10 times its weight in gold when you need to set the gap on a sparkplug.

Tweezers. A big help when trying to grab little things.

Small mirror. Sometime this allows the only way to see what's blocking a small passage, then a better diagnosis and tool selection can be made.

Torque wrench. These devices are great when a shop manual mandates a specific tightness for a critical bolt.

Strap wrench. In outboard repair, such devices make gripping the flywheel much easier. I've seen homebrew versions made with a stick of oak and an old leather belt.

A vintage ignition electronics diagnostic center on a tabletop. At left is a magnetic charger to add zing to tired magnetos. The black unit at top center is a Merc-O-Tronic tester for coils and condensers. The device beneath it does similar checkups. The handheld continuity tester (bottom right) is useful for detecting short or open circuits. Most of this gear hails from the 1950s or earlier.

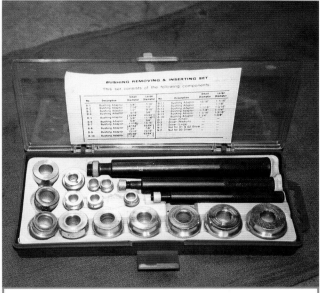

A bushing removal and insertion tool set can be useful in skilled hands.

Pipe wrench. Sometimes a pipe wrench provides the only grab that'll work, but be careful of its teeth.

Starter-spring winder. An Outboard Marine Corporation service booklet from 1954 offered the following directions for making one of these clever devices: "Simply bend the blade of a [standard slot, medium size] screwdriver about one inch from the tip. Grind the side faces [of the bent length] down to a slight taper (to fit elongated anchor hole in the pulley) then wind the [rewind starter's] spring to full 'take-up' and back off one turn. Hold pulley [with the tool] in this position while inserting the replacement starter cord." While this tool won't work on all rewind starter assemblies, it should be useful for buffs with 1940s to 1960s Evinrude, Johnson, and Gale products.

Piston-ring expander. The old mechanic's adage that "there's a tool for everything" rings true here. Although most amateur small-engine restorers simply use their fingernails, a small screwdriver, and just the right amount of pressure here and there to remove piston ring without snapping it, those who do lots of rings wouldn't be without this reverse pliers–like item.

Piston-ring compressor. Sure, a big hose clamp around a sleeve fashioned from an index card will do the trick, but some buffs like going "pro" and therefore purchase an "official" ring compressor. Someday, I'll go out and get one.

Impact driver. When all else fails in the hopelessly frozen nut or screw department, this tool can crack the job. Of course, there's got to be enough of a head on the screw and flat nut surface to get a good grip. Also crucial is the degree of impact one uses to hit (with a hammer) the impact driver case. A buddy lamented over a sharp blow that caused the tool to slip and drive a hole into the project outboard's cylinder.

Flywheel puller. Because every outboard (except electrics) has a flywheel, everyone who works on these motors should have a puller. This is a fine "first specialty tool" for one's classic-outboard motor repair shop. Wedging and prying screwdrivers between flywheel and magneto plate is a poor substitute.

Bench grinder with grindstone wheel, wire wheel, and buffing wheel. 1/4-horsepower motor is OK, 1/3 is better, and 1/2 horsepower is what some professional shops use. Extenders/adaptors are available to mate a grinding, buffing, or wire wheel to a discarded washing machine motor.

Electric hand drill. Battery-powered versions are great . . . as long as the juice doesn't fade in the middle of use.

Brace-bit driver (hand drill). In addition to the obvious use, sometimes a screwdriver bit in one of these old faithful tools can give just enough manual "oomph" to crack free a stubborn screw.

Hacksaw. After years of owning low-price hacksaws that always sprung apart at critical moments, I gladly accepted a friend's suggestion to break down and spend 25 bucks on a top-of-the-line version like the ones plumbers use. Just before I made the purchase, though, he found me a vintage, high-quality Stanley model (with three extra blades) for $6 at a garage sale. What a joy it is to saw from start to finish without popping blades and looking for the "boinged out" blade-retaining nut!

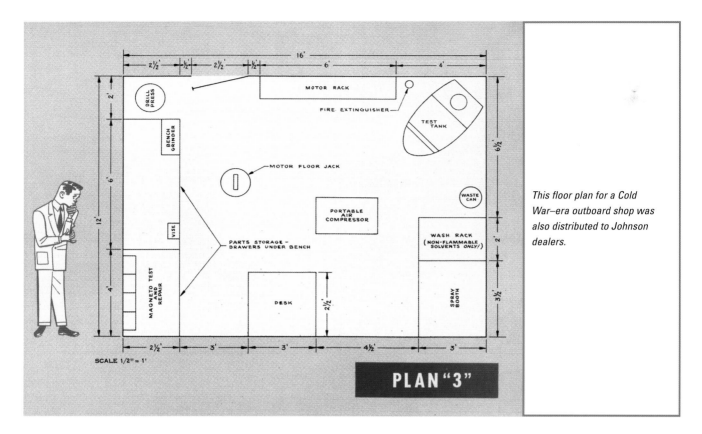

This floor plan for a Cold War–era outboard shop was also distributed to Johnson dealers.

Tubing cutter. When making new water or fuel lines, this produces neater results than a hacksaw.

Utility knife. For everything from scrapping off gasket remnants to cutting rubber fuel line. Be careful! A good one of these is incredibly sharp. Never extend its blade further than necessary.

Scissors. Collect several sizes as needed. The little ones are especially handy for making gaskets.

Tin snips. When you have to fabricate small parts or need just the right size shim, these are the best resources for accurately cutting thin metals.

Awl. As long as it's not used in desperation, the scratch awl serves a variety of a vintage outboarder's purposes, from cleaning out a tiny crevice to marking (for proper re-assembly) metal parts.

Chisels. Every once in a while, you'll need one for breaking open a tightly sealed cylinder–crankcase connection or planing off a surface to accept a new gasket.

Micrometer. (0 to 1 inch) Even those of us who aren't mathematically inclined can "mic" parts for size comparison and to determine wear.

Vernier caliper. These range from the "dollar store" plastic variety to expensive digital-readout models. They measure outer diameters, inner diameters, and depth.

Punches. An assortment of punches with pointed ends (center punch) and blunt ends (pin punch) should be appreciated for dislodging various pins and indenting parts with dots for identification. A spring-loaded model works well for the latter.

Vise. If you've got the bench room and the budget, a full range of small, medium, and large vises will prove useful. If there's only space for one, go with a medium (4-inch jaws). And, as with other tools, the higher the quality, the better. Look for an old (but not abused) heavy-duty U.S.-made model at estate sales. Be sure it can still close tightly and that its jaws aren't overly marred. High-quality models will have replaceable joining surfaces.

Tap and die set. Rare is the project outboard that doesn't have at least one stud, set of recessed threads, bolt, or nut that needs cleaning or re-threading.

Screw-extractor set. These are tools one hopes won't be required, but which are great for last resort rescues. Be advised, though, that they don't have a 100 percent success rate, and can be a challenge to use.

C-clamps. Although perhaps not priority items in the mechanical realm, put a few in various sizes from 3 inches upward on your long-range list. An electric fishing motor with a broken-off transom bracket caused me to buy a C-clamp for securing that poor little troller to the bench stand.

Drill press. My favorites are industrial-looking, circa 1940s, American-built units on big cast-iron stands. While

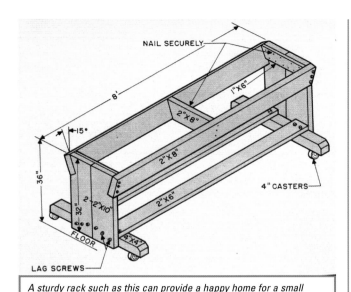

A sturdy rack such as this can provide a happy home for a small classic-outboard collection.

waiting to find one locally, I picked up a garage sale, Taiwanese bench-top-sized press for $25 that has, so far, done everything required.

Grease gun. Get one that accepts the modern grease cartridges. That'll cut down on the gooey mess of loading it. Like other tools, these should never be put away dirty.

Oil can. Either the classic pump-squirt or bottom-flex styles are neat. Then again, the commercially packaged oil tins or spray are fine, too. The key is to have spot lube at hand.

Soldering gun. You probably won't use it much, but some fussy ignition work requires such a tool. Yes, an inexpensive soldering pencil is acceptable.

Propane torch. Four of the five project outboards in this book required direct flame heat (in combination with penetration oil and muscle power) to break free a screw, nut, or bolt. Please be doubly careful with all aspects of torch use, ignition, and storage!

Flashlight. One of those small aluminum or magnesium flashlights comes in handy for inspecting dark places including fuel tanks, crankcases, and carburetors. Sometimes a light with a large head can't effectively focus its beam in tight places.

Lathe. For the outboarder possessing machinist skills, a lathe can make small parts, turn down magneto coil heels, help in crankshaft work, and on and on. "Good used" is probably the way to go. Johnson Motors used to suggest a 10-inch x 4-foot model represented a perfectly acceptable size for the small commercial outboard franchise. Our projects that called for lathe work went fine with an old 9-inch x 3-foot South Bend model.

Arbor press. In old kickers with bushings or bearings that are factory-pressed into place, the arbor press is helpful. This, however, is a tool that may be acquired as needed. It's a rarity in most basic shops, but has few substitutes.

Ignition-testing components. Devices such as the contemporary Ignition Chek unit, as well as the host of available coil, condenser, and points testers can quickly move outboard spark trouble diagnoses out of the voodoo guesswork realm. Because many old motors have some ignition ailment, such gear is worth pursuing new from an auto parts store or used from a reputable seller. Basic to this genre is a simple continuity tester and/or a volt and ohmmeter from Radio Shack. For pre–World War II outboard buffs, a magnet charger might come in handy when servicing old magnetos.

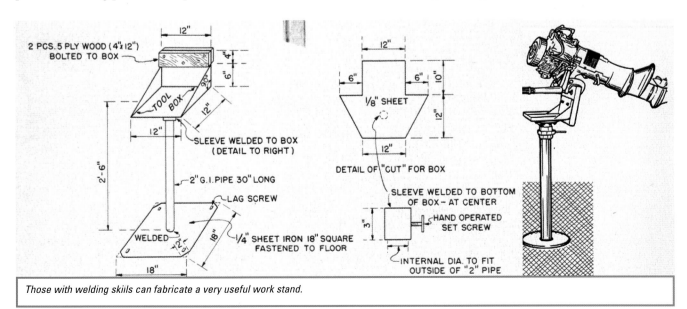

Those with welding skills can fabricate a very useful work stand.

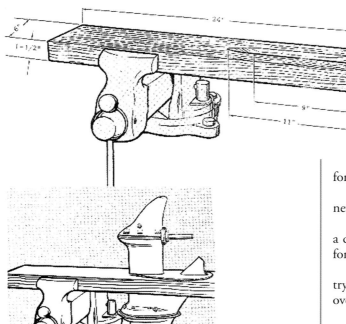

Classic outboarders who do lots of gearcase and shift repair projects will find this simple slotted fixture, fashioned from a piece of 2x6 lumber, quite worthwhile.

Parts washer. One of this book's project motors got its parts washed in a discarded baby's bathtub. Fancier units specifically intended for motor work are available commercially. The latter items are nice, but do pretty much the same thing as the kids' plastic bathtub.

Air compressor. I finally bought a second hand air compressor and related hose and fittings after getting headaches from manually blowing out water and fuel lines and passages. Another outboarder decided on a similar purchase after manually restoring fuel lines and also having a funny taste in his mouth for a week.

Bead blaster. Once primarily the province of well-financed restoration shops, the bead blaster, or sand blaster (including cabinet, viewing port, rubber gloves extending into the unit, and air-driven hose and nozzle setup), is now embraced by hobbyists who appreciate easily cleaning crud off of any part that'll fit in the unit he or she selects. Some shoot walnut shell particles instead of microscopic glass beads. A compressed air source is required to operate this restorer's friend.

Lapping block. This is simply a flat surface on which sandpaper may come in contact with a part (such as a cylinder where it meets the crankcase) that needs precise smoothing.

Level. Sometimes—such as when trying to determine if a flywheel that looked weird was really slanting a bit—I've used levels for quick analysis. They're usually accurate and never need new batteries.

Ruler. Because things sometimes just need to be measured for comparison or accuracy.

Fire extinguisher. If you have one, you'll probably never need it . . . and that's good!

30-gallon plastic trash barrel. Liner bags, a broom, and a dustpan from the local dollar store make good accessories for this indispensable receptacle.

Overhead winch. This device is a back-saver when trying to handle big motors. Reportedly, vintage outboards over 10 horsepower mysteriously get heavier every year.

Test wheels. Typically make and model specific, these propeller substitutes are nevertheless worth acquiring if often testing and tuning a motor in a tank.

Worth mentioning are special tools offered by most outboard manufacturers to their dealers. While OMC (Evinrude, Johnson, and Gale Products brands) and Mercury put the majority of these limited edition items into circulation, even obscure motor makers such as Flambeau (1946–1957) advanced their modest dealers some proprietary repair tools that made replacing some hard-to-reach components a lot easier. This legion ranged from Mercury's Quicksilver racing lower-unit water-pump impeller access socket to Johnson's tool for removing magnet rotors and gauging heel clearances on models HD-25 and TD-20.

Even though extremely handy when encountering particular outboards, most of these specialty tools would probably seldom be used by the average old-kicker buff. In the 1980s, I jumped at the chance to buy a complete set of Mercury tools from the remnants of a legendary Adirondack-area Merc dealership. Eventually, I took them to another longtime Mercury man just to have their exact purpose identified. If you do lots of work on certain models of one brand, a few of these nuance tools will come in handy. Old marine shops often provide the best sources for them. While proprietary tools often simply end up as pegboard art, I find them tough to resist if the price is right. Usually it is, as the seller typically has no idea what the things fit.

And remember: No matter how elaborately you choose to equip your shop, be sure to save an honorary pegboard hook for that favorite beat-up old wrench, pliers, or screwdriver that's been with you for years.

In addition to describing how to treat old outboard motors in need of tender loving care, this chapter is really about making decisions. That's because each step on the motor restoration stairway demands answers to the creaky question, *To what extent* shall I clean, polish, re-plate, paint, repair, weld, replace parts, and improvise? In other words, *How far shall I go?*

Even before loosening a single screw, it's best to understand that the satisfying niche between not being thorough enough, and getting completely carried away requires constant massaging. Like the dream home restorations featured on the PBS how, "This Old House," any kicker redo project possesses the power to generate fiscal overruns and emotional nightmares. My Adirondack neighbor's

This classic four-cylinder 1957 Western Auto Wizard Super Power 25 was purchased to be a "runner" and is externally clean enough for the owner to revitalize mechanically and run regularly at vintage boat meets.

Kicker Tips 4.1
Outboard Repair and Philosophy 101

Be prepared to hit a few roadblocks on the highway to your motor's restoration. The most accomplished classic-outboard repair buffs aren't exempt from this brand of potentially frustrating problems associated with diagnosing and curing ills in old and often abused machinery. They do, however, tend to look at these puzzling predicaments as fascinating challenges that can build character. That's probably why an old-outboard repair project taken on by parent and youngster (or by grandparent and grandkid) can be such a good communication and learning tool. The motor on the workbench will present many "teachable moments" and neat memories that'll far outlast any aggravation a stubborn piston ring might temporarily cause. Be positive, seek advice whenever needed, expect to learn new things, and live that old saying, "Where there's a will, there's a way."

The author encountered numerous hurdles when restoring this circa 1907 Waterman Porto. Happily, though, some of the restoration became a family project when his dad volunteered to craft the motor's oak handle, his son (then in junior high) thought to use a tuna can for the hard-to-find muffler shell, and his wife suggested the antique become a living room display.

mobile home makeover never made the famous TV show, but his lessons learned are analogous to our motor repair topic and worthy of relating here. He began by planning to put vinyl siding around the trailer's base, changed that plan to shoveling out a small crawl space for lawnmower storage, and ended up having a full cellar dug and concrete poured. Needless to say, the poor fellow didn't get 20 cents on the dollar for his efforts when he sold his mobile home on a full basement a few years later.

Unless for viscerally sentimental reasons, it's not wise to invest a winter's worth of spare evenings and several hundred dollars on a garden-variety old outboard ultimately worth 80 bucks. Before each classic-outboard project gets underway, I picture that mobile home and its conspicuous trapdoor down to the expensive poured cement recreation room. This always gives me needed perspective and has resulted in simply cleaning up and running many a rather generic old kicker that probably

Kicker Tips 4.2

On Second Thought, I'll Hold On to It

Unless a replaced part is really shot, don't be so quick to discard it. Many are the vintage outboarders who can conjure up regrets about some rusty component they tossed out but later wished they'd kept either to fit a subsequently acquired similar engine, for trading purposes, or simply because they later discovered that such a part could be refurbished.

I once purchased a 1907 Waterman Porto that was missing its fuel tank and starting crank, but came with an extra cylinder, albeit cracked and broken through the water jacket. It seemed too far gone to keep. While I figured on giving it the heave-ho, a fellow old-outboard collector offered me the needed tank and starter in exchange for what I considered hopelessly damaged extra part. He had welding skills that put the decrepit cylinder in a different light and eventually on his soon-to-be-running Waterman motor.

Parting-out is such sweet sorrow, but for a "stalk" of a motor like this, it's probably the most humane way to go.

wouldn't give two putt-putts about being some elite "hands-off" showpiece anyway.

DECISIONS! DECISIONS!

Carefully deciding what you eventually hope to do with your classic motor should help in the crucial hierarchical selection of remedies. Vintage outboard buffs may choose from the following improvement options.

Part out. This means the motor is not a likely candidate for any of the actions subsequently listed. Some of its parts, however, could give new life to some other elderly outboard of similar type. One summer at a boating museum flea market, I spotted a 1930 Lockwood Chief with a wooden dowel serving as crankshaft. Long ago, its actual crank had seized up, sending major parts through the crankcase. Three of us got together and bought the hopelessly ruined machine for $27. Its exhaust assembly went on my '29 Lockwood Racing Chief, while other parts, from steering handle to propeller, were divided among the other two buffs for their ailing Lockwoods. The rule of thumb when considering a part-out is, "The more common the motor, the more obvious the decision to strip it and find new homes for those parts." Conversely, even a stuck powerhead (albeit minus lower unit) of an ultra-rare motor, such as the low-production behemoth 1928 Johnson Giant Twin, would probably be tough for most collectors to simply part out.

Fix up. Here, a bit of old-fashioned elbow grease and whatever repairs necessary to get the old gal operating again come into play. In "handyman's special" rental real estate

terms, this motor will be put back into service after just enough of a general clean-up and repair to satisfy the local building inspector and some not-too-picky tenant. Any scuffing, scratches, hideous old welds, and big fuel tank dents remain, but simply get their surface grime wiped clean. Mixing and matching or jerry-rigging replacement parts for practicality, rather than historical authenticity is allowed in this mode, and only areas needing acute attention receive much focus. Seldom is the fixer-upper taken completely apart unless absolutely necessary.

Revitalize. The most popular route for most enthusiasts, revitalizing the motor goes well beyond just fixing up. The outcome calls for a resultant motor that the average passerby would remark "is super clean and runs so nicely!" If the piston(s) turns smoothly and provides good compression, revitalization may not always require opening up the powerhead. But everything from flywheel to propeller nut would be reduced to a grouping of parts and then undergo a bath, wire-brushing, polishing, repair (where needed, and as close to factory-original as reasonably possible), touchup, and re-assembly. That powerhead (crankcase, cylinder, and innards all intact) would get the aforementioned deluxe cleaning, too. Even so, parts that were originally nickel-plated, for example, but now show signs of the plating having peeled or worn away, would get wire-brushed and buffed to the point where the surface patina looks as if it had had loving attention. Re-plating would not be part of the revitalization process. After cleaning and smoothing a fuel tank on a motor undergoing this level of attention, the

Kicker Tips 4.3

What Antique Outboard Judges Want

As with the inspection regimen officials use to scrutinize vintage cars, antique outboards at competitive shows are subjected to a strict 100-point set of criteria. Take a look at the scoring sheet that judges at one of America's oldest annual boat shows use to determine which motor gets the blue ribbon.

• **Complete and Correct Parts?** (20 points maximum) Look for missing and incorrect size and style of screws, nuts, washers, shrouds, covers, shields, cotter pins, clamp, steering handle, levers, clamp pads, gas, valves, knobs, prop nuts, tilt pins, steering grips, carburetor, and propeller.

• **Worn, Damaged, and/or Sloppily Repaired Parts?** (minus 20 points maximum) Check for worn and damaged parts. Look for ANY rust, corrosion, modifications, gas tank dents, damaged cotter pins, "buggered" screws, nuts, washers, wires and connectors, cracks in rubber hoses, and correct hose clamps, etc.

• **Finish, Plating, Paint, and Decal Condition?** (20 points maximum) This section applies to the quality and correct application (such as proper-for-year-built) of plating, paint, decals, and buffing and polishing, as well as cleanliness of motor, including grease, dirt, dust, and even dirt in the screw slots. A motor with a very good original decal should score higher than a motor with a replacement decal, which in turn would score higher than a damaged or faded decal, which scores higher than a missing or incorrect decal. Check for correctness and quality of nickel and chrome plating, paint color(s), polishing, and buffing. Clean motors score higher. Perfect original plated or painted surfaces get scored higher than restored surfaces, which score more than scratched, faded, deteriorated, dirty, and/or incorrect surfaces. Beware of over-restored motors, as all entries should be judged to "as-from-the-factory" standards.

• **Do All of Motor's Features Work?** (20 points maximum) Check for functional (where originally so-equipped) recoil starter, gear shift, neutral clutch, auto-bailers, tilting, steering, rudder, spark advance, muffler, compression release, ignition cut-out, variable-pitch prop, electric starter, gauges, generator, wiring harness/receptacle, hood and cover latching, knobs, sparkplug protectors, spare sparkplug holder with sparkplug, remote fuel tank/hose/connector, steering bar and bracket, remote control equipment, coil box, battery, etc. Working features score higher than those that are present but non-operational.

• **Running Motor?** (10 points maximum) If a motor starts on the first attempt, it scores higher than one that fires up on the tenth pull. After starting, the engine should run smoothly, cleanly (as expected when shipped from factory), and sound "correct."

• **Presentation Presence?** (10 points maximum) A well-presented motor is on a stand that relates to its lineage and should be accompanied by original sales brochures, instruction manuals, or other supporting historic data and signage. Factory-original literature and vintage-appropriate factory or aftermarket accessories (such as oil cans, canoe bracket, tachometer, tool kit, and dealer promotional giveaway items) score highest. Spectator "ohhh and ahhh" reaction to the motor display can be positively factored. A photocopied owner's manual or parts booklet scores higher than if nothing accompanies the motor.

Notes: A perfect motor could receive 100 points, but that score must mean it is absolutely perfect with no room for improvement. This is an uncommon occurrence. Most winners score somewhere between 85 and 92 points.

This one-of-a-kind antique was home-crafted during the Great Depression by a clever mid–New York State machinist who probably never threw away any motor part. In addition to nicely fashioned homebrew water-cooled cylinders and a specially cast rope sheave plate, the 1936 Hudson River Special wore modified components from at least three different brands of outboards. By the way, in another life, the Special's exhaust pipe had been a vacuum cleaner handle!

Even though the decal is chipped and scratched, both it and the fuel tank appear to be in good enough condition to undergo a "revitalization" as opposed to a "restoration." The latter would require a replacement sticker, thus destroying an authentic 1948 Speeditwin decal.

This pre–World War II Sears' Waterwitch air-cooled 3/4-horsepower single can be an easy restoration, as all of its cosmetic parts (starter pull handle, magneto lever knob, carburetor adjust knob, and tiller grip) are intact. The red paint isn't original, but it can be removed and the motor re-sprayed a factory-original dull aluminum. Decals represent the only cosmetic challenge, although they can wait until reproductions become available or are fashioned from vinyl.

enthusiast might purchase and apply a reproduction decal. Revitalizers can also make their own with stick-on letters or computer images, as long as it stays within the spirit of the original. I saw a homebrew decal pasted on the purple brush-painted hood of an early-1960s Sears Elgin 40-horse that declared in nineteenth century English script, "Ye Olde Faithful Outboard." Nice thought, but serious collectors would give that motor mender the dickens.

Restore. Antique boat show judging committees stress that a restored outboard should appear and operate *just as it did the day it left the factory,* nothing more and nothing less. This mandate typically requires lots of serious cosmetic attention, as well as a successful search for 100 percent correct parts, right down to the authentic type of screws originally used to affix the fuel tank to the cylinder casting. Even a decal from a motor made the previous year will knock points off a restoration. The process requires the motor be completely reduced to each of its individual components, that these parts be brought back to "like-new factory" standards, and that everything then be rebuilt the way the manufacturers' employees did eons earlier. An entire evening might be spent just plating and polishing nuts that hold the tiller arm. A book filled with nice original and restored kickers is my *Beautiful Outboards,* available from www.motorbooks.com.

One warning from those aforementioned judges: Be sure that your restored motor is NOT over-restored.

Kicker Tips 4.4
Thanks for the Digital Memories

While not traditionally a province of outboard repair shops, the digital camera can be a tremendous tool around the workbench. Digital shots of your project motor before and during dismantling come in mighty handy when trying to recall how the parts are supposed to go back together. These pictures can also be emailed to other enthusiasts who'll then have better visual context to make helpful recommendations. Save some disc space for an image of the finished product, too.

Elto's 1928 Quad featured a double bank of twin-opposed cylinders. It makes for a very desirable antique, but some buffs who've found them in stuck condition never managed to free them, no matter what solvents were used in the attempts.

This 1939 Elto Handitwin restoration included such judicious returns to "from the factory" cosmetics as a coat of dull aluminum spray paint on the lower unit, muffler, cylinders, and fuel tank, as well as a polished flywheel.

A single repro decal and aluminum paint helped make this early-1940s Mercury-built Sea King a reasonable restoration. The cast-aluminum fuel tank helps, too, as it's not subject to dents, just leaks around the seam.

A close-up of the Elto powerhead shows reproduction decals and freshly worn paint on the motor rests and flywheel nut resulting from gently setting down the motor and removing the flywheel to remedy an intermittent ignition problem. The centerline of the decal accentuates a weld bead around fuel tank. Nothing is perfect!

Polishing a part that came from the factory as a painted piece (or vice versa) is a no-no. Prior to undertaking any restoration, one should fully research company literature for definitive details. Vociferous buffs waving some 75-year-old sales brochure have been known to chase officials around the exhibition area arguing that, "Yes, the factory *did* offer this motor with a copper muffler can! See, it shows one in this little picture!" Some catalogs, however, were notorious for showing artists' renditions of prototypes that looked somewhat different in actual production.

It is good to remember that, with some work, you can always move a motor from fix-up to revitalization, and on to a full restoration. Typically, this jump happens for revitalized outboards that mean enough to their owner to warrant such a reward. Interestingly, though, some buffs report having the most fun with a revitalized kicker that can be popped on a transom and used without too much concern that it'll sustain damage from transport, fingerprints, fuel drippings, curious kids, and sunlight. Unless

Kicker Tips 4.5
How Stuck Is It?

It's not all that unusual to find a vintage kicker with a flywheel that won't budge. Consider this one stuck or "set up." Such a stigma might not be fatal, but it will serve to reduce the motor's immediate market value. When classic outboarders chat about getting a motor in stuck condition, the question "How stuck is it?" is usually posed. Here are the degrees:

• **Blame it on the lower unit.** This isn't so bad at all, as the sticking usually comes from problems in the gearcase—rusty or corroded gears, seized bearings, or stubborn propeller. Freeing this end can be a whole lot easier than a powerhead kind of stuck. You can tell if the lower unit is the culprit by removing it from the motor. If the flywheel turns, the lower unit did it.

• **A little rust, a little gum.** It's possible (hopefully) that the stuck powerhead is just a case of pistons being "glued" to the cylinder walls with old fuel residue or some surface rust. Remove the sparkplugs, spray in some penetrating oil, kerosene, or plain old motor oil, let it work for several days, and then see if you can wiggle the

flywheel with a strap wrench. When it comes loose, the cylinders should be removed for inspection of the innards.

• **Severe rust and/or corrosion.** Water in the cylinders is never pretty, but is especially damaging when it sits there for months or years. Winter weather can cause this uninvited water to freeze and burst the water jacket and cylinder. This condition often promotes such rusting of cylinders and corroding of pistons that one of the only ways to extricate the pistons is by the "grease gun method." It employs hydraulic force, requires that the connecting rod be removed from the crankshaft, and isn't for the faint of heart.

• **Extreme rust and/or corrosion or pistons melted onto the cylinder walls, as well as connecting rods bonded to the crankshaft.** Any serious rust and corrosion could be from decades of moisture, but a few minutes of running without enough oil or cooling water quickly prompts friction points to heat up and seize. Most buffs pass on these problems. Some, however, try removing the connecting rods from the crankshaft (even if they have to hacksaw the rods) and then

attempt to break apart the piston with a screwdriver or chisel in the hope of saving the cylinder. Even then, extensive refurbishing is in store for that jug. If it's this stuck, one must join the Optimists Club before proceeding!

Consulting period literature can help the antique outboard restorer determine what his or her motor looked like in factory-issue condition.

stored in a climate-controlled environment and handled only by loyal servants wearing white gloves, 100-point, show-quality restored motors need restoration tune-ups on a surprisingly regular basis. This is not meant to discourage the potential classic-outboard restorer, but comes as a word to the wise wondering if they should be content to simply have a nicely revitalized "runner," or would feel happier owning a museum artifact restoration.

As counterintuitive as it may seem, most collectors agree that a motor in "nice original condition" should *not* be restored. An engine that has survived many decades without having its mechanical and cosmetic elements change much from when new, serves as a more accurate window into

history than does a restored motor wearing recently applied paint and plating, fabricated reproduction parts, and brand-new decals. Any "original condition" outboard capable of scoring 75 points or more in competition is best kept clean, properly serviced, used carefully, and otherwise left alone.

DIAGNOSIS

There's a strong temptation common to old-outboard enthusiasts. When embarking on any of the above improvement processes, we usually just want to start investigating the situation by quickly taking apart whatever looks most interesting here and there. To minimize disorder and frustration when that pile of stuff is minus something crucial

Increasingly popular with many collectors are vintage "flea-powered" outboards such as the 1/2-horse Elto Cub and its deluxe Evinrude sister, the Mate. Some might say this Cub example is over-restored, due its being highly polished (the factory just painted them an aluminum tone) and wearing a shiny blue fuel tank. Still, it looks mighty cute on that reproduction advertising display stand!

It all comes down to deciding whether you want a motor that has a finish that looks "old shoe," like the original Sea Horse 10 hood (top), or a beautifully restored motor with a sheen like that of its "after" portrait, sporting a vinyl replacement decal. Once redone, though, that trusty old Johnson didn't have as much fun, because her owner was suddenly afraid of scratches and even excess sunlight.

at rebuild time, grab a clipboard, scrap paper, and pencil before wielding any other tools. Jot down what your plan is for the motor at hand (*How far will you go?*), note parts or repair that it obviously needs, and sketch any parts relationships that you might not clearly recall a month or so down the road during re-assembly.

Along the way, use the clipboard to briefly chronicle what you did and why the action was taken. More than once, I've been very glad to be able to consult years-old scribbling reminding me which piston was replaced, where the condenser got connected, or what racing-engine cylinder is a modification of a standard-service jug. And there were several occasions when drawings of, say, how an exhaust tube was unconventionally connected *to* the lower motor cowling saved me the frustration of trying to figure out how to connect the darn thing *through* it. Chapter Five of this book was written from such clipboard notes. I've never heard a single classic outboarder complain about having taken simple notes relating to the motor improvement process. It's a good place, too, for keeping track of your project expenditures and names and numbers for parts and information leads.

Whenever feasible, get a copy of your particular outboard's "exploded view" parts booklet. These helpful documents, sometimes with proprietary servicing directions, have been gathered from defunct dealerships by Antique Outboard Motor Club members and are sometimes available for nominal copying and mailing costs. Seek them via the appropriate links on the www.aomci.org website. Anthologies of various makers' parts books are also available commercially.

Clipboard and parts view sheet at the ready, secure the subject motor to a sturdy service stand and examine it for the following:

Smoothness of powerhead action. Remove the spark-plug(s) and ground plug wire(s) to the motor. Next, when pulling the rewind starter cord or directly rotating the flywheel, feel for desired "normal friction." Art DeKalb, who served as foreman on *The Classic Outboard Motor Handbook*, suggests that when slowly rotating the flywheel and listening and feeling for powerhead problems, there shouldn't be any play, sloppiness, or clunking in the *crankshaft-moving-the-connecting-rod-moving-the-piston* action. A little play (1/16 inch maximum) in the up-and-down direction is OK. A

Kicker Tips 4.6

A Little Thing or Two from Mobil Oil

In 1950, the Mobil folks published a tiny giveaway booklet titled "Your Outboard" and focused on several "little things that count." The oil company's list is so elementary that it may seem like a bunch of no-brainers, but more that a few classic outboarders have been confounded by at least one item on this roster.

"A sparkplug wire that is loose – a loose sparkplug – a throttle or choke connection coming loose – a carburetor needle valve [and/or its packing nut] that isn't tight – a fuel vent valve that isn't opened – just little things but they can stop your engine, make it hard to start, cause you trouble at the most embarrassing moments. You can make your engine more dependable by checking these little things."

Mobil also warned, "possibly the most common cause of trouble in outboards is water in the fuel tank and what results from it. This comes from condensation. When the fuel tank is left partially full and the tank vent open, air is drawn in as the tank cools. In the same way dew collects overnight on your boat or anything else left outdoors, especially around the water, it is left also *inside* the fuel tank. It doesn't take long for enough water to accumulate to interfere with proper fuel flow and prevent starting. Sometimes it causes the formation of a soft jelly-like material that thoroughly blocks the fuel system."

Finally, the brochure discussed pre-ignition, and noted, "usually, an overheating engine [especially due to cooling system problems] will begin to *pre-ignite.* This means that as the metal of the cylinders becomes hot it ignites the incoming fuel mixture before the time when that cylinder should fire – before the spark occurs. In other words, the explosion in the cylinder occurs before the piston is ready to be pushed down by the exploding or burning gasses. The evidence of this is usually very plain from the knocking of the engine."

The owner of this 1938 Elto Pal stows the vintage 1.1-horse eggbeater in a bucket aboard his aluminum fishing boat in case his other vintage outboard conks out.

Testing for spark can be as easy as clipping the sparkplug base to something metal on the motor and giving the flywheel a good spin. A spark should appear in the plug's electrode gap. Don't pull the cord without the magneto high-tension wire(s) being hooked to the installed plug, which should be grounded to something metal on the powerhead. Otherwise, the magneto could sustain damage.

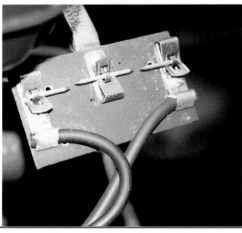

An inexpensive and commercially produced spark tester can show fire from both coils jumping the gaps on its simple component board. Wires connect to the motor's sparkplug leads, and the tester's center contact is clipped to the motor for a ground. However, open air testing can't diagnose magneto trouble caused by compression.

rough, noisy, or uneven rotation warns of broken piston rings, bad bearings, worn wristpin(s) or connecting rod(s), crankshaft trouble, and/or scored piston(s) or cylinder(s).

Cylinder compression. A generally acceptable *minimum* reading when subjecting old motors under 20 horsepower to a compression gauge is about 50 pounds per square inch (psi). Of course readings higher than 50 psi are better, and some higher performing motors from the 1950s onward are capable of psi in excess of 100. Multi-cylinder models should yield

Using a compression tester, the repair team is about to rope-over a motor to get a reading on how much compression is generated in the top cylinder. Each type and era of outboard has acceptable minimum compression, below which there's probably not enough for the engine to start. A check valve in the unit's sparkplug-hole fitting keeps the air in the gauge until a measurement can be read. Low compression could signal anything from a bad head gasket to bad rings or worn pistons. Note that sparkplug leads aren't grounded to the motor. They should be!

A piece of paper towel should be stuck into the carburetor opening during disassembly, when every orifice needs protection from foreign matter.

individual readings that don't vary by 10 psi (as compared to the highest rated cylinder). If the poor old kicker won't even deliver 40 to 50 psi, squirt some oil into the sparkplug hole, rotate the flywheel several times, and go for another reading. The oil should help make a better seal between piston and cylinder, and thus increase compression. At the very least, low numbers mean that the piston rings need unsticking or replacement. It's also possible that the piston(s) and/or cylinder(s) are not within suggested tolerances.

Spark. A sparkplug with tip attached to its high voltage lead and the threaded electrode section grounded to the motor is all that's needed to get an "open air" indication of the magneto's condition. While roping over the flywheel, look for a spark at the bottom (electrode) of the sparkplug. If there's no spark, close the electrode gap a bit and try again; occasionally this will help a weak ignition coil generate at least some spark. Never test the magneto by asking an unsuspecting helper to hold the plug wire! Yes, it has happened to me. The presence of a fat, bluish spark is a welcome sign, as it probably means that the magneto and points can take a rain check on revitalization. Still, the plug wire might need replacing or at least an appropriate end lug or boot. Even if the spark looks healthy, I like to subject the magneto to an Ignition Chek tester. This tool has helped me solve an oft-frustrating problem of seeing decent spark when testing in the open air or atmosphere, but getting nary a pop while trying to start the same motor. Ignition Chek's inventor, Richard Fuchs, remembers having an old 10-horse Mercury Lightning that would show great "fire" via the open-air spark test method, but do nothing when the sparkplugs were reinstalled. One night, he suddenly awoke at 3 A.M. with the realization that the air pressure or compression within the cylinders might be affecting the magneto's or, most probably, the coils' performance. Fuchs then "made a clear plastic body to accept a sparkplug at one end and applied compressed air to the firing end of the plug. [With the plug's electrode under pressure, but now completely visible in the plastic tube, he could see that] the nice blue arc went out at 5 psi." Fuchs had several sets of spare coils, so he tested each with his prototype Ignition Chek device, and found some that nicely lit the plugs under lots of compression.

Longtime Mercury dealer Bob Grubb says that most ignition coils from the 1950s (especially those on OMC's Evinrude, Gale Products, and Johnson motors) are now cracked and inoperative. But, "by about 1962–1963," he adds, "OMC and Merc really crossed the bridge toward longer lasting coils." Even so, about half of the condensers found in old motors are bad. Grubb recommends testing condensers if you have the gizmo to do so. Otherwise, just budget a few bucks up front to replace the all-important ignition system condenser.

Lower-unit integrity. In this exam, listen, feel, and look for roughness in the driveshaft or propeller shaft rotation. Gears may be worn or misaligned, bearings bad, shafts might be bent, and seals are likely no longer as effective as when new. Some such seals, especially those that are not right next to the bearings, can be difficult to acquire and replace. Making use of the existing seals might require thicker grease (such as Lubriplate 105) in the gearcase, as well as inspection of the lower unit for grease leakage or water entry after each outing. Wiping the grime off of an old kicker may reveal cracks in the lower-unit casting. These fissures are typically the provinces of water having

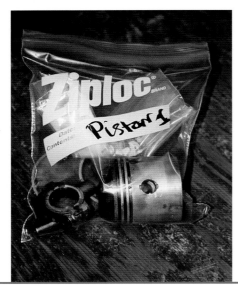

Bagging and tagging parts as they are dismantled reasonably assures their whereabouts and safety.

That's about as far as they can go. Removing the top section of crankcase on this late-1920s Evinrude Speeditwin represented a little progress, but still stalled the crew trying to remove the pistons, which were stuck in their cylinders. Fortunately, the connecting-rod endcaps unscrewed, allowing the removal of the connecting rods from the crankshaft. Then, the cylinders and pistons could be immersed in a penetrating oil bath for a possible dislodging. When the crankcase doesn't come off, the connecting rods (if there's any room between the cylinder and crankcase) have to be hacksawed. Sometimes nothing other than weapons of mass destruction will work. Bottom line: Beware of seriously stuck outboard powerheads!

frozen in the gearcase.

The water pump comes under scrutiny in this round of examinations. Unless it's a plunger-type where the up/down action can sometimes be seen, pumping efficacy will have to be determined in water. And, most veteran classic motor buffs won't take a chance on those rubber pump impellers found on the lion's share of 1950s engines. The old ones have usually stiffened and become brittle. When spun, they can easily shred into fragments that love getting jammed up into the cooling water tubes. Not only are they a hassle to remove, but the combination of diminished pumping action and plugged water passages spells disaster for the running engine. Rotating the flywheel backward on a motor with an old rubber impeller can also make it bend the other way and shear off. The best water pumps to deal with have metal impellers and usually belong to 1930s outboards. As long as nothing is blocked, they almost always work fine.

DISASSEMBLY, GROUPING, AND STORING

Whenever dismantling something during a prelude to repair, my dad always remarked that one could tell how well the thing was made by how extensively it could be taken apart, but most he stressed the mechanic's skill would be judged by how completely everything went back together. That's why, even as the first nut, bolt, or screw is removed, the classic-outboard repairer must also be focused on the subsequent task of re-assembly.

Begin by organizing a place to group the parts—each with others from its "home" area of the motor—so that they won't get lost, misplaced, stepped on, kicked, or spilled. Saving disposable food containers, such as pot pie tins, Cool Whip bowls, and TV dinner trays builds up a good stock of clean places in which to group removed parts. Also very useful are those heavier duty Ziploc plastic bags. They come in all sizes (I've fit whole small powerheads in the giant denomination) and, when closed, really ensure that whatever you put inside will stay put. Dark permanent markers make for good labeling on these parts pouches. A sturdy box (photocopier paper cartons serve well) should be assigned to hold most or all of the containers, trays, and bags filled with parts. A bed of newspaper is a good idea in the box and on the shelf, workbench, or floor area where it and large components from the project can be stored until handled again.

If starting disassembly from the motor's top, remove and segregate by group:

- **Cowling** – If any.
- **Fuel tank and associated fittings and lines**
- **Carburetor**
- **Rope sheave plate** (or rewind, if so fitted), **flywheel, and magneto** (or timer, if applicable).
- **Powerhead** – Leave as a whole assembly if examined and found to be sound, or in separately stored subgroups—

A cylinder with stuck piston. The fitting in the sparkplug base is designed to accept hydraulic pressure from a grease gun. The plate at the lower right is an example of the various covers required if cylinder ports are not sufficiently blocked by the stuck piston; otherwise any grease pressure will simply dissipate through the porting.

Sometimes, grease forced into the sparkplug fitting slowly moves stuck pistons enough to finally remove them. And, wow, is it a messy procedure!

pistons/wristpins, connecting rod/endcap, etc.—when engine is completely dismantled. If breaking down the powerhead, be sure to draw a diagram of how it looks while all together, and to identify the pistons (top, bottom, left, or right), as well as the specific endcap mates and orientation in relation to their particular connecting rod.

• **Lower unit** – Typically from just above the cavitation plate on down to the gearcase and skeg.

• **Transom clamp and tower housing**

There are occasions when stubborn screws, nuts, or bolts require the influence of direct heat (via propane torch) with a careful, well-ventilated squirt of penetrating oil or a hit with an impact wrench. Last resorts call for nut-cracking tools or drilling out the offending fastener. On each *Classic Outboard Motor Handbook* project motor, we left the tower housing firmly clamped to our "operating room" engine stand until all of the more romantic parts were safely categorized and stowed away. Keeping in mind the Biblical observation, though, that "the last shall be first," this component grouping should be number one in line for the next process.

CLEANING THE PARTS

With the transom clamp and tower housing pieces dismantled as far as needed for cleaning (and possible repair later), it should be cleaned immediately so that it can again serve as a foundation for the rest of the outboard's components. If straight, still smoothly threaded, and otherwise in decent shape, there may be no need to remove the thumbscrew pads and thumbscrews. (Bent thumbscrews can be gently tapped with a mallet to get them back in line.) The pads

All of this rusty dirt and scale came out of that little fuel tank after a single upside-down jiggle. There was more where that junk came from, too. Suffice it to say, tank cleaning is a patient person's game. For tanks with seemingly eternally problematic interiors, some enthusiasts use a "sloshing compound" that sets a fuel-proof coating on the tank's internal walls. Most motorcycle repair shops carry this stuff.

Flywheel puller in place, a Martin 200 flywheel is about to be properly removed via a twist of the wrench. Some old motors have built-in flywheel pullers that leverage a ridge on the flywheel nut against the crankshaft opening in the rope sheave plate. When a mechanic's helper is on duty, he or she may be asked to slightly lift the motor by the sides of the flywheel while the mechanic delivers a mallet blow to the loosened flywheel nut. Do not try to pry off a flywheel—this technique can result in damage to the motor and mechanic!

Lonely, dirty work that cannot be avoided. With a plastic basin, in this case a discarded baby's bathtub, partially filled with solvent, a devoted outboarder braves sub-zero winter temperatures in an open garage and carefully degreases each part of a motor he plans to revitalize before spring.

You're gazing at genuine carbon "gook" stuck to struts on a cylinder's exhaust ports. The shiny surface in the background is the piston. All of that stuff needs to be removed without knocking any of it into the cylinder.

PB Blaster was successfully used to free up the difficult-to-loosen parts in some of our project motors. Tri-Flow came in handy when we wanted to more easily replace hoses onto fittings or tiller grips onto their steering arms.

can be tough to get off and might not snap back into their swivel too well. Be advised, however, that several small metal foundries friendly to classic outboarders cast reproduction thumbscrew pads. Again, the www.aomci.org website is helpful here.

Emptying any active fuel or antique "goo" from the fuel tank is a good early step. If the tank has been empty for a long time, it will often have a dried-fuel-and-rust scale that must be completely extricated or it will clog the fuel filter screen, lines, and/or carburetor during the first trial run. Begin the cleaning process on a dried-out tank by shaking it wildly enough to prompt stuff to exit through the filler cap hole. Some folks put pebbles or hex nuts in the tank to act as agitators in this routine. At this stage, rinsing with

Flywheel integrity is crucial for safety and proper motor operation. Check the entire unit, especially its underside near the hub, for cracks, excessive keyway (slots inside the flywheel center hole and near the top of the crankshaft) wear, or warp. (Be careful not to drop the key that is wedged into these cavities.) All rivets need to be secure in their seats. Magnets can be tested for strength by seeing how much pull they have on a nail or a screwdriver. Pre–World War II magnets will most likely need a recharge.

Kicker Tips 4.7
That &%$#@ Carb!

Some of the most common motor-operation complaints outboard dealers of the classic era would hear from their customers were related to the carburetor. Frustrated folks would bring their outboard to the shop and weave tales of woe, being stranded in the middle of the lake, and confusion about just "how long to keep turning those little adjustment knobs on the carburetor?" OMC's Gale Products Division tried to help their franchisees (Buccaneer, Gale, etc.) put the issue into perspective with this handy chart. Almost every carb ailment can be troubleshot via this 1950s service bulletin.

MOTOR FLOODS:
Choke improperly adjusted
Float damaged
Dirt between float needle and seat
Float level set too high
Float valve stem bent so valve can't close
Damaged needle valve or valve seat
Dirt prevents leaf or reed valve seating
Damaged leaf or reed in valve body

MOTOR IS STARVED FOR FUEL:
Water or foreign matter clogging passages, jets, and screens
Float valve corroded or gummed so that valve does not open properly
Float level set too low
Float valve stem bent and does not open properly
Float hinge dirty or corroded
Vapor lock

POOR CARBURETION:
Jets, needle valves, screens, and fuel lines dirty
Loose connection or ineffective gasket (especially between carburetor and crankcase)
Faulty butterfly valve or choke
Dirt prevents leaf or reed valve from closing
Broken or damaged leaf or reed valve

gasoline makes sense but *not* with rocks or nuts! Often, second rinse of household rubbing alcohol will eat away any remaining resins. When the tank is completely dry again, the nuts or stones can be given a go-round. Just be sure to do it in a well-ventilated yard.

What to use for degreasing and cleaning parts can be a very touchy subject. Soap and water are the safest bet, but a grimy old outboard has a lot more dirty nooks and crannies than does the average crusty lasagna pan. Some industrial-strength detergents can do the trick. Ask the auto supply store clerk for the buzz on latest or best-reviewed stuff, and then squirt away. Except for its points, avoid getting the magneto wet, especially with water. Instead, dab the coil(s), heel, and other parts with a rag wetted with your chosen cleaner. If you're leaving the powerhead intact, don't introduce water into its intake or exhaust ports. Parts that do get a water-based treatment need to be dried quickly and rubbed with a lightly oiled rag to give the metal some rust protection. It's amazing how fast that enemy of metal can form!

Solvents designed to cut serious rust, corrosion, and petroleum-based "gook" come in a wide variety. Charcoal-lighter fluid works for some. Gumout is another favorite. Some buffs swear by a product called PB Blaster, a spray-on, penetrating catalyst with a good reputation for loosening the rust and nefarious junk that otherwise prevent easy dismantling. Of course, there are other similar products on the market, each a favorite with classic outboarders to whom it has provided success. Experimentation is the way to go. Folks not given to trial and error, though, still rally around a tub of gasoline, kerosene, or other fuel that quickly eats the grime, but yields fumes, and potential fire

or explosion. This method *must* be used outside and away from flammables and sparks. There was a rustic boat shop near my family's summer vacation spot. The old motors and the mechanic there would have been a joy to regularly visit, but even as a kid, I was leery of the fellow's ever-present cigarette dangling ashes inches above the shop's gasoline-filled parts-washing basin.

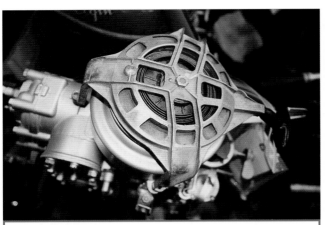

A "snake" spring gives a rewind starter its return power. This example on a late-1940s Johnson looks pretty simple and tame behind its cage.

The underside or business end of a rewind starter reveals the mechanisms that engage corresponding catches on the flywheel when the starter cord is yanked. Loosening that center screw can be the ticket to hours of frustration and mechanical adventure.

"Here, put this rewinder together." Few steps in the outboard repair process involve as much of a conundrum as redoing a rewind starter unit. There may be no universal technical advice for this project, but patience, perseverance, and three hands will always come in handy.

Saltwater and rust make this early-1970s Evinrude Mate a tough motor to dismantle. It's a good candidate for an application of penetrating oil that can be left to do its work for a week before the motor is re-treated with more, left another few days, and then put to the wrench.

Some vintage racing engines, such as this 1955 Hubbell SR with Quicksilver lower unit, were run on a fuel mix of alcohol and castor oil. If you're lucky enough to find an antique "alky" racer, be advised that castor oil residue locks up nuts, bolts, and screws like super glue! Lacquer thinner can help dissolve this stubborn stuff.

One useful technique I do imitate, though, is that bucolic technician's habit of saving old toothbrushes and paintbrushes for whisking the glop from parts that are given a bath. Regardless of the "secret formula," the object being cleaned should be taken down to the bare metal or clean-painted surface. Whatever liquid you elect to use for cleansing, don't make a practice of slopping it all over the many environmentally sensitive areas that government officials who need to fill out stacks of triplicate forms would like to catch you "impacting." This includes your own property.

After the serious dirt, rust, and corrosion are gone, a wire-brush wheel (mounted on a bench grinder's shaft) can make quick work of more tenacious stuff. Be sure to wear eye protection and beware of "spent" wires shooting from the whirring wheel. Hold items to be wire-brushed (including screws, washers, and nuts held with needle-nosed pliers) in such a position that if they get away from you they won't whip around the wheel and shoot at your face, a window, or anyplace else you're hoping remains whole. Some folks bring this operation outside. The only disadvantage to a non-confined space is the possibility of sending some precious carburetor component flying into the next county! Steel wool can also be an effective way to clean and polish parts, but avoid using it to scour the inside of a flywheel, as the strands tend to be attracted to the flywheel magnets. When hundreds of steel wool remnants become magnetized, they're mighty tough to completely remove. Beware of steel-wooling the carburetor, as well, as the tiny metal hairs can get lodged into fuel jets. None of that stuff is desired in cylinders, either.

The cleaning process provides ample opportunity to check each part for excessive wear, cracks, or outright breakage. Give the flywheel several close inspections for integrity. Make sure it's not cracked—especially in the hub area—to the point where it could fly off the motor. Use a screwdriver or nail to determine flywheel magnet strength. If it offers enough attraction to definitively pull the metal object, it's likely powerful enough to work in concert with the magneto to make spark. While a generalization, for parts subject to friction, the smoother the condition you find it in, the better. Determining the extent of external wear depends on what the motor looked like originally. For example, the sand-cast lower unit on our Comanco outboard project engine looks rather rough, but these bargain-priced motors left the factory that way. Remember: Don't endeavor to over-restore.

COMPONENT REPAIR OR REPLACEMENT
There's a strong likelihood that your shop clipboard has sustained several notes and some fingerprint smudges during the dismantling and cleaning activities. Especially, in this section, those observations require answering the question of how far this project should go in fixing existing

Decades-old parts made of low-grade alloy or "pot metals" have a tendency to be cracked or broken. This late-1920s Tillotson carburetor serves as an example: A crack is clearly visible on the edge of its choke knob. A few small foundries make replacement parts.

The Atwater-Kent ignition timer for a 1928–1929 Elto Speedster. The pot metal bushing that encases the point-trip timer cam (the disc with the protrusion) is often found broken and seized against the cam. Long-idle motors with battery-ignition timers should not have their flywheels rotated until one is sure that the timer isn't stuck. Replacement bushings are sometimes available from antique outboard buffs with a home machine shop.

parts or acquiring new (when available) ones. Screws, nuts, washers, and bolts that are bunged-up could need smoothing or replacing. These little guys get a lot of attention from judges of restored outboards, so if a prizewinner is desired, each of the aforementioned must look like a factory original. That means not replacing a brass screw with a stainless steel type, a roundhead with a flathead, and *ad infinitum*. Major antique auto restoration supply houses sell mini plating kits that use battery current and chemicals to make plated surfaces "new" again.

The rubber "starfish" impeller in this water pump body should spring its arms straight out when removed from its case. Impellers that stay bent are ripe for replacement.

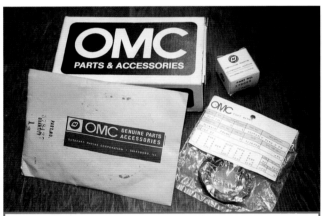

Unopened vintage stock parts are always good to have on hand, but some components, even though not yet used, have a definite shelf life. This is especially true with some ignition parts and with rubber or plastic items.

Buffing and polishing can achieve some pretty nice results on a formerly faded or dull finish. This buffing wheel is attached to an adapter on an old washing machine electric motor. Check the Internet for establishments, such as the Eastwood Company, which deal in buffing and polishing supplies.

Technically, "buggered-up" fasteners can be used if they still possess enough of a head or slot to be tightened. Even so, they won't pass muster with judges examining a vintage motor entered in a classic boat show.

For anybody who enjoys touching the past through fixing up or restoring vintage equipment, the path traveled on that journey largely depend on: (1) the person's skills, (2) how much fixing is needed, (3) whether or not replacement parts are available, and often most important, (4) how much they cost. Some items on vintage outboards that are commonly treated to replacement are:

- **Ignition coil(s)** –Mostly on post–World War II models
- **Ignition condenser**
- **Gaskets**
- **Seals**
- **Bearings** – Where available
- **Lower-unit gears** – Mostly for racing engines or mistreated gearshift-type motors
- **Tiller grip**
- **Decals** – When available

Up close, the end of this rusty crankshaft looks useless, but it will clean up on the wire wheel. As long as there's no major pitting or scratching, the piece can be made serviceable.

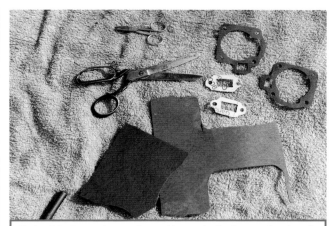

Tools of the home-shop gasket-making trade. Don't try saving ripped or worn gaskets. Instead, cut new ones from tracings of originals. If the original is not available, trace the part itself onto gasket paper.

- **Piston rings**
- **Piston(s)** – If available

The average old-outboard redo project doesn't require new pistons (unless they're hopelessly scuffed, worn, out-of-round, or have a hole burned in them), but it might well include a regimen in which the pistons have their skirts polished, their ring grooves cleared of carbon, and their domes wire-brushed to eliminate carbon deposits. A piece of broken piston ring acts as a good scraper for the piston's ring channels. Cylinders (inside) that are scored or rusted need to be refurbished to attain good compression. Carbon build-up in the cylinder dome and ports has got to go. Picking at it and scraping away this baked soot is the basic procedure, but the knife or screwdriver used to do this should not impact the smooth cylinder bore. Tools for re-boring and honing badly scuffed cylinder walls offer the cure, but require expertise. This is an area that I prefer to "farm out" to the local car repair shop or experienced small engine mechanic or machinist. Removing rust and scale from water jackets around the cylinder, though, can be done by almost anyone with perseverance and patience. Tapping the cylinder with a dowel or other object should coax rust and scale particles to exit, and freeze plugs may be removed to gain better jacket access. Compressed air blown into the water jackets is also a good way to convince the stuff that it's not wanted.

Gasket hole–punching tools eliminate the fussy job of cutting screw, bolt, or stud holes with scissors. A set of these tools is a worthwhile investment and should last a lifetime.

REBUILDING AND RE-ASSEMBLY

Using the transom clamp and tower housing as a home base, you may next attach the re-assembled lower unit and then the powerhead (or vice versa). Typically, the remaining order includes: propeller, exhaust/muffler, carburetor, magneto, flywheel, water tubes, steering yoke/tiller, fuel tank, fuel line, and applicable cowling. Actually, it's probably most logical to re-assemble the motor in reverse order

Every outboard re-assembly should begin with the transom clamp unit, on which everything else can be remounted.

For small, delicate parts undergoing repair (such as this water pump body), scrap wood serves to soften the bite of vise jaws.

Notice the nut resting against the stud and the carburetor body. The carb will have to be pulled out slightly from it reed valve case mount in order to get the nut started on the stud threads. Be prepared for the nut to drop a time or two.

Left: A pair of needle valves just removed from old outboards. The one at right needs gentle straightening. Both require cleaning. Right: "Needle Valve Horror Story" could be the title of this picture. This needle valve was screwed so tightly into its seat so many times that ridges were worn into the valve end. Consequently, fuel has little chance of being properly metered.

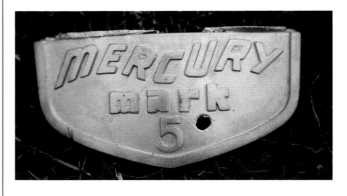

During the re-assembly process, oil (or grease, if appropriate) parts that will be subjected to friction.

This otherwise nearly impossible-to-find Mercury Mark 5 front-cover medallion was cast in a home foundry, as was the cache of small reproduction replacement pieces in the pile. Raw castings must be machined or cleaned of excess metal before installation. Such dressing can take hours.

Kicker Tips 4.8

"If your motor won't operate properly, check the following…"

Packed with every 1946–1954 Martin outboard were operating instructions that featured a page of simply explained troubleshooting tips.

MOTOR LOSES POWER:
Fuel too rich (so motor slows down)
Fuel too lean (so motor backfires and slows down)
Improper gas/oil mix
Cooling system or pump inlet plugged

STIFF (TO TURN OVER) MOTOR:
Rust in cylinder
Crankshaft bent
Propeller shaft bent
No grease in lower unit
Propeller fails to revolve
Shear pin broken
Drive on propeller shaft broken
Propeller nut loose
Rubber slip clutch of prop hub loose/broken

FUEL-RELATED PROBLEMS:
No fuel in tank
Air vent closed
Fuel shut-off valve closed
Fuel line clogged
Carburetor dirty
Tank filter screen dirty

NO SPARK:
Wires disconnected
Breaker points fouled
Breaker points do not come together when flywheel is revolved. For Martins, set at .020
Breaker points do not separate when flywheel revolved
Sparkplugs dirty, cracked; gap not set properly. For Martins, set plug gap at .030

MOTOR MISSES:
Fouled spark plugs
Broken or loose wire
Poor wire insulation
Short circuit due to moisture or oil
Breaker points corroded, improperly spaced, or fouled
Weak condenser or coil
Dirt or other foreign matter in carburetor
Fuel line restricted
Water or dirt in carburetor strainer/filter or in other carburetor parts
Bad compression
Piston rings fouled and stuck in piston grooves
Cylinder and/or piston scored/damaged

MOTOR MAKES POOR PROGRESS THROUGH WATER:
Propeller blades bent
Rope or anchor dragging
Fouled prop

HOT MOTOR:
Water pump inlet fouled
Lack of proper oil in fuel mixture
Use of wrong propeller
Lack of water in inlet tube
Worn pump (impeller) rotor
Motor not deep enough in water

MOTOR VIBRATES:
Poor ignition
Bent/fouled propeller
Clamp screws not tight
Improper carburetor adjustment

KNOCKING MOTOR:
Flywheel nut loose
Worn piston
Worn Cylinder
Worn bearings

---

of its earlier disassembly. Here's where that clipboard journal will receive rave reviews. Notes like "Long slope of the piston crown sloped down to exhaust ports" are reminders that will eliminate the kind of confusion that only gives the project a 50-50 chance of striking gold.

Admittedly, not everything will always come together flawlessly the first time. If yours is anything like the projects chronicled later in this book, lower-unit gears won't simply hop back into a smooth meshing relationship and copper water lines will seem to have shrunk or expanded a quarter inch, which makes re-threading them onto their fittings a real puzzler. And the flywheel-to-crankshaft keys will suddenly disappear from their storage container. Such challenges, however, generate the brand of experience needed to not only improve the old motor's condition, but to build personal confidence and new skill sets for the next

An Antique Outboard Motor Club member produced these small repro vinyl decals. The www.aomci.org website links buffs to these labor-of-love replacement parts services.

This homebrew decal was made with stick-on lettering and auto-detailing strips. It dresses up a revitalized motor until a more authentic reproduction becomes available.

Sheets of reproduction fuel tank decals of the water-applied type. Some restorers recommend letting these decals dry for two weeks after application, then masking the tank to within ⅛ inch of the decal, spraying the decal with a light coating of clear lacquer, and giving it a second coat after the first one dries. When the masking is removed, the lacquer should protect the decal from water and fuel.

Would you believe paper? Fire up your computer and that sign-making software, hit "print," glue your creation onto the motor, and gently coat it with clear lacquer. This design was interpreted from a tiny picture of an original in a 3x5-inch 1939 brochure.

mechanical adventure. Things almost always look brighter when that vintage outboard is all back together . . . and miraculously, no parts are left over.

THE COSMETIC TOUCH

Excepting decal application, attention to cosmetics isn't a grand finale. Painting parts, individually or in appropriate groups, is best done a step prior to re-assembly. Many old-outboard components were factory-painted a dull aluminum color. No matter what the original hue was, though, spray lacquers in acceptably matching varieties can be found at one's local auto parts store. Bent coat

hangers or other stiff wire can be used (in a properly ventilated location) to hang parts on a rafter nail where they can be sprayed in every direction and left out of harm's way to dry. Painting procedures for old outboards follow automotive bodywork guidelines. It's wise to consult the directions on the can, too.

Above all appearance-wise, a vintage kicker with a dent free integral fuel tank primarily gets positive notice for the remarkable condition of that ever-prominent part. Unfortunately, few old motors are found without a beat-up tank. Remedies include the now discouraged, for obvious safety rationales, compressed air or water high-pressure expansion

This delicate vinyl Sea Horse repro decal was created using a computer program and laser cutting jig.

The eye is drawn to the metal Evinrude badge, which fared very well since first being fastened to the gas tank in 1948. Attention should be given, though, to those starting and lubing instruction decals on the front cowl. Someone with a set of originals loaned them to this outboard's restorer for a few hours. He quickly ran them over to a copy shop, had several color copies cranked out, and glued them on the Evinrude. He'll keep the extra copies in case he finds another similar kicker in need of beautification.

This restored 16-horsepower Johnson is about to get a paint touchup, as a few hours of use discolored the upper portion of the exhaust motor leg. Whenever possible, use high-heat paint for such applications.

The Neptune logo on this World War I–era rowboat motor is indeed faded, but some buffs might argue it's too good of an original to destroy by covering it with a reproduction or repainting. The rear of the fuel tank features raised lettering bearing the maker's name, Caille. Such durable logos are favorites among collectors.

The well-preserved decal on this uncommon 3-horse, 1955 Evinrude makes one think twice about trying to restore the dented tank. Some show judges like nice originals better than restored motors.

This full mechanical and cosmetic restoration is complete with a good paint match to the original "Sea Mist" green, a bright-red, new old-stock (thus not chipped or cracked) plastic fuel cap, vinyl repro decals, and a reproduction tiller grip.

A pair of Truman-era Johnson Sea Horse 10 outboards, one an "as found" runner, and the other a fully restored show winner. Both operate well, but the one on the left isn't as pretty. Guess which motor has more fun on the water because her owner isn't particularly worried about a new scratch or two. By the way, the left-most round adjustment knob on each motor's front control panel doesn't move nor adjust anything. Johnson simply cast them into the shrouding to balance the appearance of the other two real knobs. One buff marred his trying in vain to "free it" with Vise-Grip pliers!

Even the remote fuel tank for this original-condition Champion 16.5-horsepower twin is in remarkably unscathed shape. The seldom-run motor won a first-place ribbon in an antique outboard show, but would have to have its water pump and impeller checked before being taken for a spin on the lake.

method; banging out dents, where accessible from the fuel cap opening, with a broom handle or similar metal objects; using body filler to hide the depressions; and cutting open the tank for excellent accessibility. The last technique is the most aggressive, because it subsequently requires a corrective weld and grinding the excess welding "bead." Once peeled open, however, the tank dents can be hammered relatively smooth (no more than 1/16 inch from "perfect").

Auto body filler compound utilized for smoothing is followed with successive grits of sanding (from 220- to 400-grit papers) prior to giving the tank a trip to the polishing wheel. Those who've taken a fuel tank through this process commonly report 20 to 40 hours of labor. With those estimates in mind, many classic outboarders hunt for a project motor with a decent tank, or they decide not to let nicks and dents bother them.

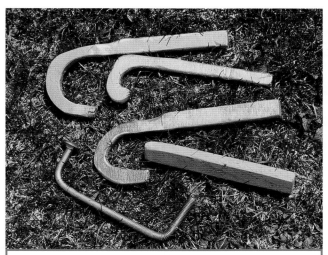

"By hook or by crook" might be the battle cry of any classic outboarder fighting to smooth out dents on a fuel tank. These implements, ranging from a piece of wood to a bent bolt and three roughly cast aluminum hooks, are used by one revitalizer to knock out tank depressions. They're intended to be introduced through the gas cap opening.

This tank was sawn in half, undented, and then welded top-to-bottom. Now, it has a date with the grinding wheel. Before starting this process, the classic outboarder must be certain that no gas or fumes are present.

Sometimes old-outboard fuel tanks look like the Yankees just used 'em for batting practice. "As long as this one doesn't leak," said one tired restorer, "I recommend calling that smashed tank 'experienced' and using it as is, or finding a smoother replacement." Investing lots of time to beautify a really lumpy tank on a relatively common old outboard is counter-productive when a replacement may be quickly found.

Some skilled outboard restorers cut to the chase—right through the tank. With such a flap, it's easier to reach the backsides of pesky dents. Once the dents are history, the flap can be welded shut and ground down. There are still hours of fussy work left to make any scars from the pushed-out dents really disappear. The motor's flywheel usually covers the flap weld.

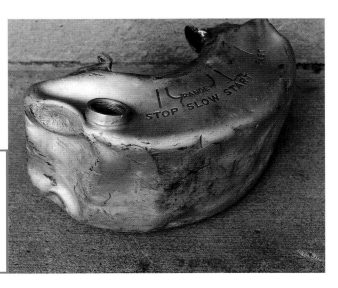

CHAPTER 5
RESTORATION CASE STUDIES

REDEFINING THE LAST WORD IN EARLY-1920s OUTBOARDING – 1922 JOHNSON MODEL B

Nobody is certain why one of the industry's first "built for saltwater use" outboard motors spent its first 80 years near the widest, deepest, and most pristinely fresh waters of Lake Champlain. As a kid, I noticed its lower unit protruding from the rafters of an old garage with a moss-covered roof. Several decades later, I happened to get another look. Serendipitously, this vintage Johnson hadn't moved an inch. Much to my delight, the flapper-era kicker came my way after her generous owner figured the 2-horsepower opposed twin might enjoy book fame better than 80 more years of hanging around.

Johnson Waterbug (also known as Ligh Twin, and both names predating the company's Sea Horse moniker) serialized B 2613, was crated for shipment from the company's South Bend, Indiana, plant circa March 1922. Johnson production had begun only about five months earlier with an "A" designated model numbered in the low 500s. Some of these very early A motors went to seacoast residents who later complained that the salt quickly corroded the otherwise

Wise old King Solomon said that without a vision people will go astray—or at least get discouraged and give up. Being able to realistically imagine our long-neglected Light Twin...

...as a beautiful princess instead of a frog was the key to staying focused and following through on this project.

The 1922 Johnson Lightwin or Waterbug, as found. It had just emerged from spending an indeterminate number of years in the rafters of an old Adirondack camp's garage.

Model designation and serial enumeration are stamped into the flywheel's rope sheave plate. A three-digit serial number denoted one of the first Johnson outboards made; #2613 is still a very early motor for this now-famous brand. In addition, it was manufactured quite early in Johnson's B (or saltwater) series.

Some manufacturers stamped a model and serial verification on their motors' crankcases. Ideally this stamping will match the one on the rope plate. Matching numbers indicate the rope sheave is original and that this one is really B 2613.

well-received lightweight aluminum components. "B" versions, with salt-resistant drive and propeller shafts, were rushed to market, while tiny decals proclaiming "This is a fresh water motor only" were stuck on the fuel tanks of A Waterbugs and Lightwins. Literature indicates the B fix involved a nickel-over-brass driveshaft housing, similarly nickel-coated screws below the waterline, and stainless steel shafts "with a cross ground into the end of the prop shaft." Curiously, our B is equipped with bronze shafting. Typically, a good test of "official manufacturer" authenticity (as opposed to a nicely executed homebrew modification) is the existence of at least three identical examples. So far, one other bronze shaft B has surfaced, leading me to speculate that they're representatives of the factory's earliest foray into saltwater motors.

Months before putting a wrench to this outboard-industry milestone motor, I envisioned it becoming one of the "working" favorites in the collection assembled for this book. As a potential runner that could be easily transported, displayed, and taken for a spin around the lake at

Antique Outboard Motor Club meets, this little guy became an obvious candidate for a nice, laid-back revitalization, as opposed to a full restoration. That way, this B Waterbug could have fun on the water again, instead of being relegated to fussy storage in some proverbial glass case. Of course, no classic-outboard project plan gels until tempered with an initial motor checkup and diagnosis. Here's how Johnson B 2613 fared:

• Compression generated 50 to 60 psi, an acceptable minimum for a powerhead of that size and vintage and with dry cylinders and pistons.

• No connecting rod rattling or audible or tactile signs of related wear.

• Cast-aluminum fuel tank (as opposed to formed sheet metal) not subject to denting. However, it did sustain some nicks.

• Motor is complete (except for missing muffler tubes, carb air-intake horn, and tiller grip) but had the following problems:

1. Magneto/stator plate was from a later motor.

Examination of a recently acquired vintage outboard should include assessing the level of wear and denting on major external components such as the flywheel and rope sheave plate. These scrapes and dings are pretty typical.

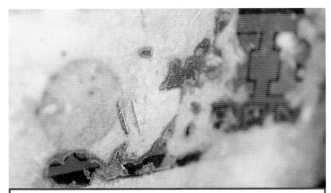

Divots along the rear of the fuel tank represent the worst damage to this cast-aluminum tank. They really aren't too bad at all, but will need to be filled with auto body compound if a new decal is in the plan.

Mangled screw heads, such as this one affixed to the gearcase casting, require replacement if a full restoration is to be undertaken, or simply cleaned up with a file if the motor is to get a fix-up or revitalization.

As a teaser for how the motor could look as a nicely revitalized or perhaps even a restored piece, the rope plate gets the initial treatment on the wire wheel. The wheel removes much of the tarnish, but deep scratches are still quite evident.

2. No spark.

3. 3/4-inch hairline crack found on flywheel rim.

4. Slight wobble detected in flywheel's outer diameter while looking down at the powerhead and rotating the flywheel.

5. Lower-unit gears sounded a little "lumpy" when slowly rotating flywheel.

6. Steering yoke was cracked near mounting bracket. One elbow was owner-fashioned from plumbing pipe-fitting.

7. Water-input fitting on driveshaft tube looked "factory," but was actually a plumber's street elbow connector.

Because none of these were major caveats, and due to the fact that the powerhead was judged to have decent compression, nice piston "bounce," and clear water jackets (nothing loose flaked out, and air blown through the water

The plate is then subjected to a sanding wheel, where the heavy scoring is rubbed out. Care must be taken not to cause gouging. Hand-sanding follows and improves the surface that was "rough-smoothed" via the heavier grit paper on the sanding wheel. Finally, the rope plate gets its turn on the soft buff wheel.

A section of the nickel-plated torque tube is rubbed with a Scotch-Brite type of kitchen scouring pad, followed by a quick test application of Simichrome polish, which gives the project team encouragement.

fitting on the cylinders demonstrated a free flow), we decided to revitalize the old Johnson without breaking open the crankcase or removing the cylinders. The motor's relatively low operating rpm and the location and small size of the flywheel crack prompted us to use the existing flywheel. Had cracks been noted in the hub area, another flywheel would be mandatory.

An opportunity to swap stator plates for versions from the correct year was accepted, but spark in this "new" one was nonexistent, too. After cleaning, points disassembly and re-assembly, condenser replacement, and reinstallation, the process yielded no juice and had to be reprised—three times! An electric points-testing device (that in retrospect should have been utilized for the first go-round) showed

Removing and turning over the flywheel provides access to the steel hub, magnets, points cam, and lead counterweights. A good de-rusting is in order.

The Johnson B minus its flywheel. This was the first time the team noticed that a corner of the steering rail was actually a plumbing fitting—a nice fix, but not factory-kosher.

Early Johnson carbs can be slipped off by loosening a single screw.

This spark advance lever was taken from a motor similar to the project engine, but one that was used in salt water. Check out the corrosion! Fortunately, our B was void of such deterioration.

That @#!%$#* screw! First we tried a screwdriver alone, then wrench leverage on the screwdriver shank, and then penetrating oil with the process repeated, but nothing happened.

A torch heated up the screw and drew in more penetrating oil so that the screw finally budged. Of course, care must be taken with solvents and fire. Appropriate venting is crucial, too.

Some projects are filled with roadblocks of this kind. Severely deteriorated nuts and screw or bolt heads must be approached with logic, patience, and strength. Happily, the method shown here did the trick, although the screwdriver slipped a couple of times.

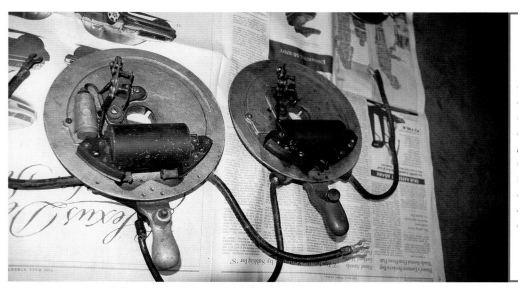

While thinking about how to approach a problem fastener lodged in the lower unit, we began considering the magnetos and related mag plates. The one found on the B (right) didn't actually belong on the motor. An earlier magneto assembly was located and a swap answered the diversionary dilemma.

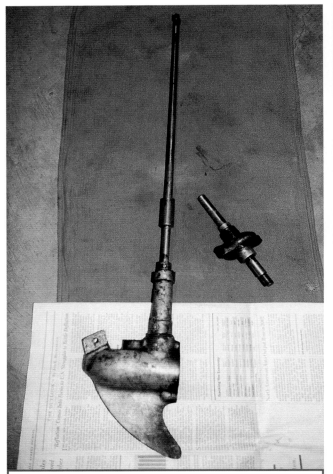

The lower unit with propeller shaft and related gears removed. As of this writing, the jury was still out as to whether the bronze shafts were Johnson factory products or the clever work of a skilled home machinist or Johnson dealer. Period literature indicates the B was built with stainless steel shafting.

This small electric filing tool creates a dimple in a stuck driveshaft fastener so a drill can be positioned. Gripped between wooden blocks in a vise, the driveshaft assembly better accepts the drill. Once a hole could be drilled in the headless screw, an extractor backed it out. Sometimes things don't go so routinely.

bad point contact, even though everything looked fine to the naked eye. Simply roughing-up the points with a bit of sandpaper did the trick.

Removal of the propeller shaft cap and inspection of the gears showed little gear wear. Fortunately, the roughness in the gear action was due to poor mesh relationship, and the gearcase's "lash" or take-up adjustment would later get the gears happily back together again.

Finding an original replacement for the aforementioned water-input fitting on the driveshaft tube took a couple of weeks and delayed the project's grand finale. An original-style reproduction decal had been ordered and made it to the shop mailbox well ahead of the water pipe part. Meanwhile, each piece of the "B," including its intact basic powerhead assembly, was soaked in solvent, brushed free of grease and dirt, rinsed in kerosene, dried, and then wire-brushed. Next,

With the bad screw removed, a tap cleaned the threads in its former bed while a new screw was custom made on the lathe. Total time from the start of the removal process to the insertion of the replacement? About 55 minutes. No wonder some restoration projects take months!

Old paintbrushes, wire brushes, toothbrushes, and rags were used to scrub each piece submerged in this solvent. Rubber gloves staved off the frostbite that doing this job on a 10-below-zero January morning can produce.

Because this powerhead had good compression and it didn't feel as if any internal components were noticeably worn, it was not further dismantled. Note the cloth stuffing designed to keep out dirt during degreasing and wire-brushing.

components were set out on newspaper and arranged according to each particular group's parts (water pump in one zone; gearcase, gears, and shafts in another; and so forth) in a handy location on the shop floor. The transom bracket was mounted on the shop stand and became home base for the re-assembly process.

Excepting the ignition mystery, the only other challenges in putting the old Johnson back together occurred when:

• The water tubes didn't seem to want to line up for threading onto their cylinder fittings;

• The fuel line at the bottom of the carburetor got kinked when we tried to fit it over its new air intake horn, and it had to be gingerly re-curved;

• A pair of muffler tubes resisted the first 45 minutes of attempts to mate them to the inside grooves of their respective exhaust manifolds; and

• It was realized that we forgot to grease the water pump plunger prior to installation, necessitating the pump's disassembly and lubrication.

The shop crew joked that this old outboard didn't cause nearly enough trouble to be a poster motor for Murphy's Law, but remarked just how much effort—even without having to get into the crankcase—the six eight-hour revitalization sessions took to do a careful job on B 2613. Nevertheless, with celebratory mugs of hot coffee in hand, though, it was agreed that the 1922 project engine sure

After their bath and a trip to the wire wheel, the cleaned parts are laid out on newspaper.

First to be re-assembled is the transom clamp and torque tube, as it will host the rest of the vintage Johnson. Art DeKalb puts the gearcase into place. Art's tentative smile is probably the result of drive gears that, for a good part of a half-hour, wouldn't go back into place. Suddenly and without any explanation, however, they finally decided to snap "into gear." Things often happen that way on these projects. Note that Art's protective mask, which he used while at the polishing wheel, is at the ready. Prior to polishing the motor parts, the mask was white. Better that stray stuff gets on the mask that in the lungs.

looked nice. And further cheers went up when the kicker obliged to possibly sputter on its second pull, and then truly sprang back life, for the first time since the early 1960s, with the next yank of the starter cord.

To be fair, a gas leak should be mentioned. Common to many a newly redone motor, the fuel lines, shut-off valve, and connection to the carb aren't sufficiently tight, or their gaskets are missing, misshapen, or improperly aligned. It's also not unusual for the needle valve packing (gasket) to leak, or for the float level (on its float pin) to be improperly set in such a way that fuel to a full carburetor bowl can't be temporarily interrupted (as intended) when the float has fully risen. Any of these conditions can cause annoying fuel drips or outright flow.

The plunger-type water pump in pieces. Check valves and plunger all had lots of remaining life, and that old spring still has ample "boing."

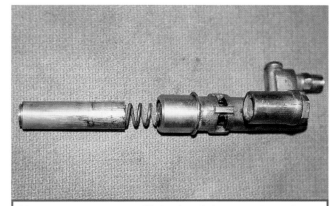

The water pump is re-assembled and ready for remounting on the motor.

The freeze plug was pulled from the cylinder end long ago to check the condition of the water jacket. New freeze plugs don't cost much—a penny fits like a glove! This cylinder is from a 1924 motor, so the collector revitalizing it went to a coin show and found a penny from that year.

For illustrative purposes, the team cracked open another early Johnson twin. This simple and effective design revolutionized 1920s outboarding.

The cleaned-up powerhead is reattached to the torque tube.

Most of the rust shown earlier is now gone, and the flywheel is nearly ready to crown the crankshaft. A nearly vertical hairline crack was discovered on the flywheel's outer face, but was determined not to be a threat to the motor's operation.

The correct magneto and plate. It's OK to reuse wires and plug lugs in a revitalization like this, as long as they're not cracked.

As is often the case in most classic-outboard rebuilds, we had to fabricate some replacement gaskets for the Johnson B.

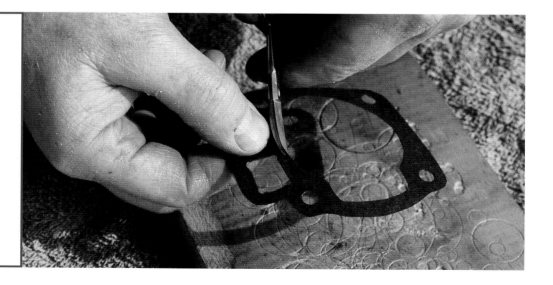

It required a whole morning's worth of work, but the motor's fasteners and fittings are nicely cleaned, buffed, and de-bunged.

This view of the carburetor float bowl shows the pincher float-pin catch. The pincher grips a groove around the pin to achieve the proper fuel level in bowl. Sometimes the pincher jumps the groove, but it can be reset via sight and/or feel.

A toothbrush is required to clean the surface and crevices of this carburetor, which is shown at right, dismantled and post scrubbing.

In this motor's case, the screen filter in the fuel line–to-carburetor body fitting prevented a sure coupling. When repositioned, it was discovered that the two mating surfaces (on carburetor body and fuel line fitting) were not completely flat and therefore wouldn't give a complete seal even with a gasket. To correct this, each surface was rubbed along sandpaper placed on a flat piece of metal. With each part to be mated truly even, a fine seal occurred and the leak stopped.

The motor continues to take shape as more parts are added.

Each thread in the powerhead is subjected to a tap for sure cleaning and re-threading.

For convenient rotational filing and hand-sanding, the flywheel is placed on a cut-down crankshaft end in a lathe.

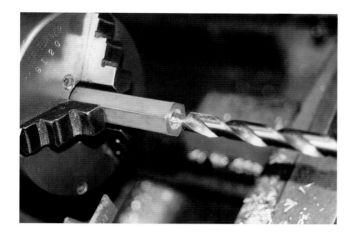

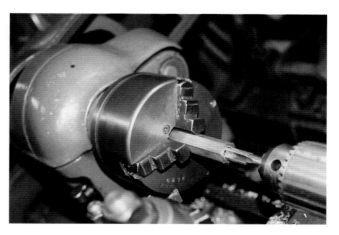

For the Johnson B we had to machine a brass gear lash-locking nut not available at the local hardware store. After some brass stock is drilled in the lathe, its threads are tapped and the piece is cut to Johnson reproduction specifications. Following a few turns of the buffing wheel, the new nut that will go on the B gearcase is complete.

The fuel tank is being buffed and polished out of doors because of the dust it produces.

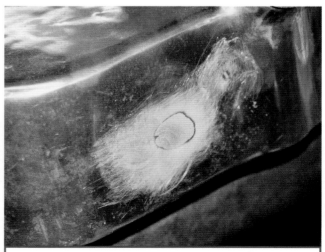

Deep dings are roughed up and treated with auto body filler. A decal will cover this blemish.

A week later, hand-sanding removes most of the now-dried filler and scuffing.

A bit of a setback. The motor is done except for its decal and tiller grip. Pulling the starter cord, however, reveals no spark. The tester shows that the points are not making requisite contact. The naked eye indicates otherwise, but we trace the circuitry and go through the magneto again anyway.

The ignition points are sprung open by hand and its components dismantled for the last time.

Roughing up the points on the sanding wheel was the answer. When re-assembled, the magneto generated a fat spark.

A vinyl reproduction 1921–1922 Johnson decal is applied. This is very fussy work and can be ruined if the sticky parts of the decal touch each other or if it isn't applied in such a way that all of the air bubbles can be worked out. Sometimes the only remedy for air pockets is to gently pop them with a pinpoint and try to lay the pucker flat.

The revitalized and mostly restored Johnson Waterbug glistens in the April sun.

This reproduction rubber handgrip replaces the original's leather covering. Still, the new one does the trick.

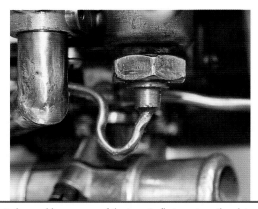

Prior to her maiden voyage of the twenty-first century, the vintage Johnson was fueled up but immediately developed a leak where the fuel line and carburetor fittings meet. Sanding these surfaces flat and making a spongier gasket solved the oozing problem.

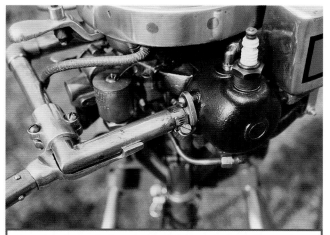

A crack in the handrail necessitated the use of a hose clamp to keep it sturdy. A rail in better shape—and minus the plumber's elbow fitting—was located and scheduled for installation on the motor the following winter.

The author, outboarding in front of his Oswego River home in Upstate New York, happily steers the Johnson-powered craft away from shore. The smooth sound of the old kicker makes the long winter's project well worthwhile.

A 1950s OMC CLASSIC GETS THE ROYAL TREATMENT – 1958 SEA HORSE 10

What red-blooded boating buff with young sons could pass up an outboard that's reminiscent of the motor once on his boyhood craft? When New York Finger Lakes region resident Dick Curvin spotted a "For Sale" sign on our subject Sea Horse 10, he instantly understood the familiar-looking 1958 twin needed some TLC. It was stuck and the cylinder head was literally hanging by the sparkplug wires.

After Johnson model QD-19, serial number 1703480, was rescued from the flea market, its new owner figured the stuck pistons to be only lightly lodged. He freed them with a generous dowsing of penetrating PB Blaster and some coaxing from a strap wrench. Curvin also knew that most 1950s Outboard Marine Corporation products require a new set of ignition coils and condensers. However, even after such a replacement, the Sea Horse 10 performed more

As found, the 1958 Johnson Sea Horse 10 appears to be in pretty good shape, cosmetically speaking.

Under the hood things look clean. There is surprisingly little powerhead paint fading or wear. This shot was taken after the cylinder head had been re-bolted to the cylinder assembly and the motor "unstuck."

Disassembly begins. First, the rewind starter is removed, followed by the carburetor control panel with its easy-to-lose cosmetic screws, knobs, and springs. Note the spare shear pins and cotter pins taped to the tiller handle. That's sometimes a good sign that the motor's former owner was conscientious.

We get to the carburetor and things still look well maintained. Lots of linkages, tiny fasteners, and wire hose clamps make careful disassembly and parts storage crucial. Be careful not to pull off hoses in such a way that they break.

like a 5-horse machine. With the motor rattling at low speed and unable to achieve anywhere near its full rpm, Curvin got out his compression tester; it showed 65 psi in one cylinder and 75 psi in the other. Even the higher reading was about 10 psi shy of decent compression for a relatively modern classic.

The seller emphasized that the Johnson hadn't endured many hours of use. A closer inspection of the powerhead indicated that, while this claim might have been accurate (the engine compartment paint still looked new and shiny), internal noises and the questionable psi and rpm probably pointed to someone early on having been recklessly skimpy with the Sea Horse's oil prescription of a 1/2 pint per gallon of gas. Consequently, the pistons, cylinder walls, connecting-rod bearings, and wristpins were likely victims of friction wear that's capable of sapping lots of horsepower. Perhaps the fatigue was a blessing in disguise, as the motor seemed to inexplicably jump out of gear while underway.

A strap wrench makes loosening the flywheel nut an easy twist of the wrist.

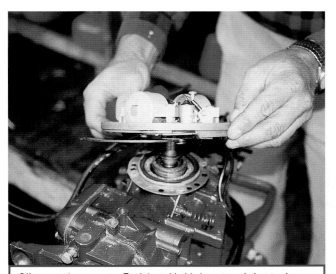

Off comes the magneto. Truth be told, this is a staged shot to show disassembly order. The actual mag had a coil coating that dried out and cracked, typical of a 1950s OMC mill.

Permanent markers can be useful to identify which end of what went where. Jot down further reminders on your project clipboard. Note the washer and spring on the crankshaft protrusion. A few words on that clipboard about their proper placement will later jog the memory.

At the dock, gearcase lube was noticed oozing from the lower unit. An offending crack there was patched, but the shifting problem persisted. From top to bottom, this classic screamed for help! Curvin opted for an extensive revitalization with further plans for a cosmetic restoration later on. Getting it to run like a lively 10-horse became the first priority.

In about an hour and a half, the 1958 Johnson was reduced to dozens of parts. Each component, except for the lower unit, which turned out to be from a 7-1/2-horsepower model, was cleaned and assigned to a waiting supply of Ziploc food storage bags and plastic containers. Evidence of scored pistons, worn piston rings, and bad bushings in the connecting rod convinced the shop crew that its clipboard "to do" list would be getting longer.

During the rebuild, new rings were installed on pistons, which had their domes wire-brushed and sides polished. One ring wouldn't completely seat until some microscopic carbon particles missed during scraping were extricated with a knife.

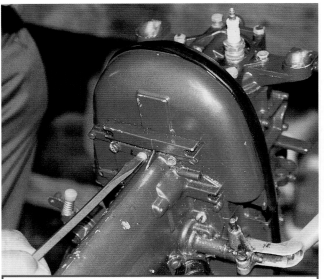

This stubborn powerhead-to-motor cowling screw required penetrating oil and additional force from an adjustable wrench attached to the square screwdriver shank. Make sure the screwdriver you use securely fits the screw slot.

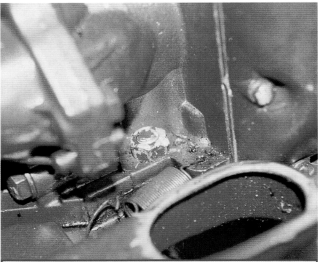

The revitalization crew spent 20 minutes removing the innocent-looking (vertically positioned) nut in the middle of this picture. As is often the case with at least one fastener, access was the problem. The sides of an open-end wrench had to be ground down in order to get the tool onto the nut.

Before the aforementioned wrench mod, frustration led us to try knocking the nut loose with the blow of a screwdriver to one of its corners. Hey, kids, don't try this at home.

Bushings for the offending loose connecting rod/piston wristpin joint were not readily available and had to be made in the lathe. They served as an example of how a project can be slowed several hours for lack of a small part or two.

Next, the inside of the cylinder head was wire-brushed. The crankshaft felt smooth with no pitting or scratching noted, so it received the greased needle bearings and connecting rods and the related pistons. A replacement rubber O-ring in the top (crankshaft) bearing appeared to be too loose to act as a seal there, but compressed acceptably when the crankshaft was placed in the back section of the crankcase. Considerable difficulty was experienced when trying to get the top and bottom bearings to simultaneously seat in the "keeper" pins protruding from the crankcase

With all the nuts and screws out of the way, the powerhead can be lifted off of the tower housing. Even at this early stage of opening up an outboard, it's best to be careful not to get dirt into places that are supposed to be free of such matter.

The Classic Outboard Motor Handbook *mechanic and his patient. Art DeKalb holds the Sea Horse 10 powerhead just prior to its visit to the workbench for "open-part surgery."*

bearing bed. It was tough to tell if they were properly seated until the smaller crankcase shell could be fitted into the equation. The fourth try resulted in good fortune that continued when we slid the cylinder block onto the pistons as if they'd sorely missed each other's company.

With the powerhead re-assembly accomplished, satisfied smiles emerged—until it was discovered that the crankshaft refused to rotate 360 degrees. A connecting rod was hitting the inside of the cylinder block and casting a dangerous level of discouragement on the project—it was even suggested we throw the thing out of the widow. Luckily for the frustrating mill, we were in a basement, plus an elderly neighbor phoned at that instant seeking help to get his escaped cows back into a barn. The bovine distraction provided just enough of a temporary refocus to approach the Sea Horse with a better attitude and the determination needed to break down (gasket sealer and all) what had only recently taken a rather tense hour to build. As suspected, the lower connecting rod was inadvertently installed backward on the piston. It was one of those things that looked right, but wasn't.

Once the powerhead was correctly rebuilt, it was mated to the transom clamp bracket and tower housing. A local used-outboard parts garage had been put on the lookout for a proper circa 1958 10-horse lower unit, but came up empty. Instead, one from a 1961 model was borrowed and matched to the project motor. Challenges in this phase resulted when we attempted to connect the gearshift linkage and match the water pump tube to the piping through a small access port

For secure positioning, a period OMC service manual suggests gripping in a vise an old driveshaft that'll mate to the female crankshaft fitting. That's what was done to hold this powerhead upright and make it accessible.

That's a clean machine! The just-removed carburetor manifold shows an encouraging like-new quality. The gasket on the reed plate (still affixed to motor) has adhesive splotching, but can probably be reused.

in the motor leg. This took place well after lunch on a Saturday in November, when we were fully cognizant the summer home's shop being used for Phase 1 of the Sea Horse revitalization was imminently slated to be closed for the season. In fading daylight, the Johnson was placed in the test tank, fueled, primed, and roped over. Tension cut through the crisp fall air, as pull after pull yielded nothing. Someone noticed that the choke hadn't been activated. As soon as it got some choke, the motor sang out. After shutting it down to see if the Sea Horse could be restarted reliably, subsequent cranking enlivened the engine with hardly a foot's length of the starter cord. What had only recently been a bunch of plastic bags filled with parts was now churning up the test tank water. QD-19 1703480 demonstrated smooth operation from high-speed to idle. Its only abnormal noise was a slight bit of piston slap at extreme idle.

The internal side of the reed plate reveals reeds that act as valves to let the fuel mixture into crankcase but not out.

A knife is used to scrape away small remaining particles of gasket and old gasket adhesive.

The bypass port cover is removed to allow a quick peek at the top piston and rings. A bit of rust is noted through the center port, but it doesn't appear to be serious, at least from this limited perspective.

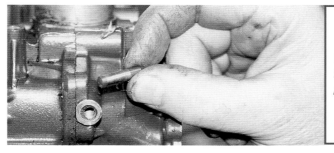

This taper pin is one of several on this motor used by the factory to align front and rear sections of the crankcase. They are gently tapped out with a punch and mallet. Don't lose even one of these little necessities!

The front portion of the crankcase is separated from the crankshaft bed. Even if you have a copy of the motor's shop manual, get out your project clipboard to note the positions of O-rings, washers, springs, and bearings along the crank. The crew agreed that this mill seemed mighty tidy. Still, there remained the matter of discovering why it had run so poorly.

The motor's new owner saw this cylinder head at the time of purchase, as it was hanging by the sparkplug wires. Gasket looks OK, but the domes are sufficiently "carbonated" to require a good cleaning.

Lifting the top bearing off of its bed reveals the O-ring channel (sans O-ring) and the hole that seats into a corresponding pin when assembled.

Note the smooth condition of the crankshaft journals, which ride in the bearings. They won't require much attention in this project.

An Allen wrench is employed to remove the connecting-rod endcap screw. Because these screws were snugly fit at the factory, they take a bit of pressure to crack.

The connecting-rod endcap has been removed, revealing the needles that are lined up on the piston section of the connecting rod. These needles are parts of the needle bearing assembly. Caution! Don't lose any of the needles or drop them into the powerhead. Have a Ziploc bag ready.

Prior to cracking the crankcase, the team took a few minutes to observe piston and cylinder condition, and to determine whether the water jackets around the cylinder were in good shape. A bit of scale needed to be scraped from the cooling jackets, but the presence of factory-original paint inside the jackets is a positive indication that this engine hadn't seen saltwater use.

With the needles safely stowed and the endcaps repositioned on their related connecting rods, the pistons can be pulled and stored as one assembly. Note the tiny depression (visible on left connecting rod) where the endcap mates to the connecting rod. The manufacturer put that there to indicate how the matched parts must be assembled. If there are no marks, make some and jot down instructions on your project clipboard before you remove the endcap!

The pistons relax outside of their cozy metal home for the first time since Eisenhower was president. They'll soon undergo inspection and the team will determine whether to use them for another term in the motor.

A team member checks the cylinder bore condition with a little help from a wall lamp. Turning the cylinder assembly at different angles should help reveal any carbon deposits, scoring, or scratches. This one looked OK.

"There's your trouble!" A portion of each aluminum piston sustained this level of scoring. Interestingly, their corresponding sections of the steel cylinders were not significantly damaged. The team determined that these pistons could be smoothed and reused. Had the motor been destined for lots of future use, as opposed to 10 or 15 hours per season as part of the owner's vintage outboard menagerie, new pistons would have been sought.

The Sea Horse 10's piston rings were stuck in their grooves enough to prevent them from properly contributing to engine compression, a probable explanation for the outboard's poor performance.

With the piston ring repositioned in the cylinder (without the piston), a feeler gauge measures for the factory-recommended width for healthy rings. The rings were quickly designated for replacement.

With the piston removed, the piston wristpin is shown in its connecting rod and bearing. It wiggled in the bearing enough to indicate that new bearings were in order. It's likely that some of the engine noise was caused by the poor fit of the wristpin in the worn bearing. Because factory-replacement bearings were elusive, a set was fabricated on the home outboard shop lathe.

The guilty bearing with its rubber O-ring sits next to the fasteners that held the pistons onto their wrist pins. Specially nosed pliers are available from auto parts stores to make it easier to grip these fasteners. The needles from the needle bearing are surrounded by a piston ring that's destined to be broken and used as piston ring groove scraper.

After they are subjected to the segment of old piston ring, the ring grooves or channels are cleaned with a file.

Powerhead a la delicatessen packaging. With disassembly and examination assessments complete, most of the motor's parts are stored and marked in food containers and bags. This, and several pages of notes on the project clipboard, will come in very handy down the road (and in a different shop) when the revitalization resumes.

The new piston rings are in place, and they exhibit springiness far superior to the old ones. Note the tiny pins in the top and bottom ring channels to prevent the rings from rotating. When you replace the rings, be sure not to cover these protrusions. While the cleaned-up piston skirts shine brightly, the incredibly stubborn carbon deposit blotches on the piston crown survived wire-brushing.

Look Ma, no ring compressor tool! Dirty fingernails are a sure sign of do-it-by-hand determination, as a project team member shows us the magic touch required to compress three rings while gently sliding the well-oiled piston into its waiting cylinder. Remember that specific pistons go into specific cylinders a specific way. That's why proper marking and good notes are wise.

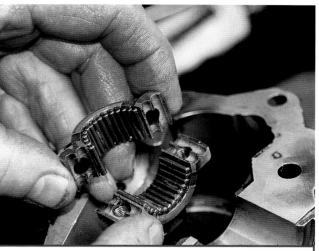

With the pistons in place, the connecting-rod endcap areas get a grease coating needed to receive needle bearings. Lubriplate 105 was used here, but any good automotive grease will do.

Don't nobody sneeze! That thin layer of grease holds these two rows of needle bearings in place. Soon they'll be safely circulating the crankshaft journal. When you do this, be certain all of the little needles are accounted for, as the absence of just one will negate the project's effectiveness.

A clean shop rag or fresh paper towel should assure that no dirt, sand, or dust gets onto the oiled crankshaft during reinsertion. Note that the rubber O-rings on the top and bottom bearings are already slid onto the crankshaft. The springs in background also fit into the mix. Yes, we had to look at our shop clipboard more than once during this stage of re-assembly.

Fitting the bearings, crankshaft (while wiggling it onto the connecting rods), O-rings, and springs into the anxious crankcase took three attempts. Each time, as cool heads prevailed, it got a bit easier.

The front section of the crankcase. Note the bronze center main bearing for the crankshaft. It had sustained remarkably little wear.

Before the crankcase halves can be properly re-bolted, the locating pins must be hammered into place. They serve to align the two halves so that no undue binding occurs.

Snugging the crankcase bolts. If the crankshaft is harder to turn when the bolts are tight than when they are loose, something isn't properly aligned.

The cylinder head after a thorough wire-brushing and cleaning.

A gasket-sealing lubricant is applied to the water jacket and cylinder assembly surfaces.

Tightening the head bolts. Consult your shop manual for the proper torque rating of these fasteners, or at least be sure they're all equally snug.

The underside of the powerhead is prepared with a sealant near the cooling-water passageway connection.

Easy does it. Classic Johnson owner Dick Curvin slowly reacquaints the re-assembled powerhead with its "mainframe" tower housing and belly pan. Note the hoses and wires that need to be juxtaposed so as not to get caught in the works.

As long as the communication is coordinated, four hands (and eyes) can prove better than two.

With the powerhead and carburetor in place and secured to the tower housing, this old outboard is ready to receive a few admiring glances—and its magneto.

The ignition timing cam is returned to position on the spring and crankshaft.

Oh nuts! Missed during examination, a crack was noticed in the timing cam during the final engine re-assembly. The team decided it could live with the hairline fracture, but described the fault on the motor's service tag.

A close-up of what some call the "universal mag" due to the fact these OMC ignition units were used on literally millions of motors from the 1950s onward. Points, coils, and condensers are still available from some well-supplied marine and auto parts retailers. Life is too short to fool with a faulty magneto when replacement components might be on a store shelf a few miles away.

The new magneto, in its place of honor, sits ready to be crowned with a flywheel.

This rear view shows the reinstalled flywheel, the related spark-advance and spark-retard linkages (brass), and sparkplug wires. The latter would have been quickly replaced had they not tested free of electrical leaks and shorts.

This wallowed driveshaft bearing in the lower unit offers another sign that our motor's bottom end isn't up to snuff.

Danger, Will Robinson! Lower-unit trouble spotted! This crack in the gearcase housing likely resulted from trapped water and freezing temperatures, a bitter recipe in the old-outboard hobby.

Two views of the Johnson's chewed-up drive gear tell the team that the motor's lower unit has had a tough life.

Compare the old water pump impeller (right) with its replacement. The essential resiliency for drawing sufficient water is long gone in the used piece.

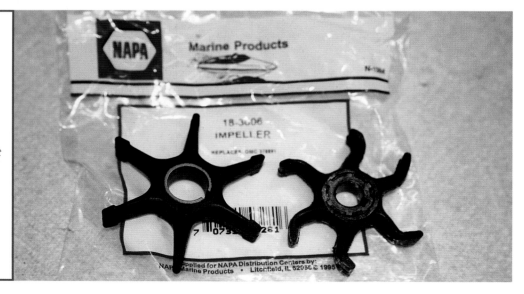

The team discovered that the 10's lower unit was previously replaced with one from a 7-1/2-horse model. That mismatch and the replacement unit's crummy condition convinced the crew to find a suitable unit from a parts motor. Here is just what the doctor ordered from a 1961 version.

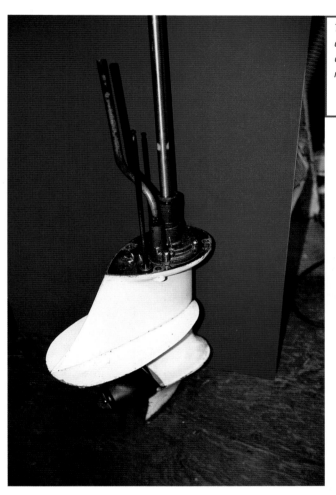

Ports on the tower housing's side provide access, albeit tight, to linkage-mating locations.

Fitting the driveshaft, shift linkages, and especially the cooling-water tube into their respective receptacles is a fussy task. Don't be discouraged if it takes a half-dozen tries.

GEARCASE GROUP
MODEL QD-QDL-22-22F-22S

1961 *Johnson*

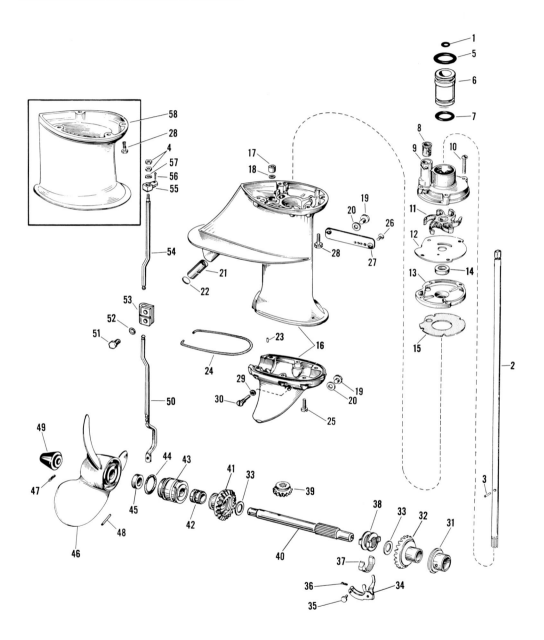

SPECIFY MODEL AND SERIAL NUMBER OF MOTOR WHEN ORDERING PARTS

12

This service manual diagram details parts for the lower unit used on our QD project motor. These drawings can really clarify what goes where and help determine whether any parts are missing.

Parts Catalog

ITEM NO.	PART NO.	NAME OF PART	QTY.	BIN NO.	ITEM NO.	PART NO.	NAME OF PART	QTY.	BIN NO.
1	303067	O-Ring	1	____	34	303340	Lever	1	____
2	307755	Driveshaft	1	____	35	302504	Pin	1	____
3	300771	Pin	1	____	36	306376	Cotter Pin	1	____
4	306556	Nut	2	____	37	303381	Cradle	1	____
5	301967	O-Ring - Top	1	____	38	377458	Shift Clutch Dog		
6	305304	Spacer	1	____			Assembly	1	____
7	302035	O-Ring - Bottom	1	____	39	307752	Pinion Gear	1	____
8	302497	Grommet	1	____	40	305261	Propeller Shaft	1	____
9	305302	Impeller Housing	1	____	41	307754	Gear - Rear Reversing	1	____
10	303395	Screw	4	____	42	303998	Bushing - Rear Reversing	1	____
11	377178	Impeller Assembly	1	____	43	377187	Gearcase Head and		
12	305303	Plate	1	____			Bearing Assembly	1	____
13	377186	Bearing housing and			44	303360	O-Ring	1	____
		Bearing Assembly	1	____	45	303345	Seal	1	____
14	303345	Seal	1	____	46	377635	Propeller	1	____
15	303339	Gasket	1	____	47	305296	Cotter Pin	1	____
16	376775	Gearcase, Bushing &			48	307949	Drive Pin	1	____
		Pin Assembly	1	____	49	305394	Nut	1	____
17	303332	. Bushing	1	____	50	305319	Shift Rod - Lower	1	____
18	301877	. O-Ring	1	____	51	304024	Screw	2	____
19	307551	. Screw	2	____	52	301551	Lockwasher	2	____
20	307552	. Gasket	2	____	53	303794	Connector	1	____
21	303331	. Screen	1	____	54	305321	Shift Rod - Upper	1	____
22	300314	. Plug	1	____	55	303702	Connector	1	____
23	300611	. Dowel Pin	1	____	56	306376	Cotter Pin	1	____
24	302622	. Seal	1	____	57	303701	Lockwasher	1	____
25	304071	. Screw	6	____					
26	302681	Screw	2	____			**MODEL QDL-22 PARTS THAT DIFFER**		
27	304579	Cover	1	____			**FROM MODEL QD-22**		
28	307151	Screw	4	____					
29	304083	Washer	1	____	2	307756	Driveshaft	1	____
30	303358	Pivot Pin	1	____	6	305552	Spacer (QDL)	1	____
31	303380	Bearing - Front	1	____	28	307151	Screw	4	____
32	378179	Gear & Bushing Assy. -			50	305408	Shift Rod (QDL) - Lower	1	____
		Front	1	____	58	303672	Gearcase Extension		
33	303361	Thrust Washer	2	____			(QDL)	1	____

Indented part names indicate that these parts are included in preceding assemblies

---- NOTE ----

Part No. 378267 Extension Kit for
Conversion to QDL-22

For Page 11 for additional Model QDL-22 parts.

ORDER ALL PARTS FROM YOUR JOHNSON SEA-HORSE DEALER

Looking more like normal. The rebuilt Model QD is ready for a compression reading and a spin in the test tank.

Who needs Webster's Dictionary to define "happiness"? Art and Dick beam as the revitalized classic outboard purrs. It sounded much better and had more rpm than before its trip to the motor hospital.

Following a successful November run on one of New York's Finger Lakes, the newly redone Sea Horse 10 will be treated to touch-up paint (that replacement lower unit needs to be matching maroon) during some peaceful, no-breeze afternoon the following spring.

RESTORATION CASE STUDIES

REDOING A DO-IT-YOURSELFER – 1958 COMANCO KIT

Posh yacht club members might snicker that they would *never* own a no-name outboard even if you paid them. But such folk probably never perused a 1956 ad in *Popular Mechanics* in which the president of Continental Manufacturing Company actually offered $30 hourly remuneration to those willing to purchase and then build one of his firm's "full 2-1/2 horsepower" kickers. Small print, however, revealed that Continental wasn't really offering to put new people on its payroll, just save the purchaser 30 bucks an hour over the full retail price of a factory-built outboard for each of the two hours spent at home assembling its do-it-yourself kit motor. Knocked-down, it sold for just $59.95 and was dubbed the Continental "Speed Kit," not because the ad promised "up to 8 miles per hour cruising speed," but due to the rapid construction warranty.

Like some of this book's other subject engines, this Kit was pulled from a flea market vendor's bargain pile of mangled motors at an Antique Outboard Motor Club meet. A fellow collector noticed the 22-pound, rough sand-cast motor, remembered me talking about needing a low-end example for this book project, offered the seller $35, grabbed the engine, and fired off a joke email stating that I had five business days to get the Kit off of his property. His communiqué's kidding mandate was a direct result of the fact that most buffs don't consider such outboards to be very significant. It was for this very reason that I chose the Kit with its simplistic, air-cooled powerhead, a project motor anyone can afford and feel comfortable playing with to learn some basics.

Our example of the Kit is stamped #8379, which probably means it's the 379th motor of Continental Manufacturing Company's 1958 output. (Or maybe it's Number 837 from 1959?) By then the firm had shortened its name to Comanco, an identity just barely legible on this motor's scuffed-up ID plate. Coincidentally, as the project was getting underway, a midwestern classic-outboard enthusiast happened to send me an original *Kit Outboard Motor*

This is just what the new outboard Comanco Kit owner would have found in the shipping carton in 1958. Instructions suggest laying out the pieces on newspaper in order to see if everything was shipped, and to familiarize oneself with the components of an outboard motor. The team on this project noted paint wear and evidence of weld repairs on the fuel tank. Somewhere along the way, the cast tank must have leaked.

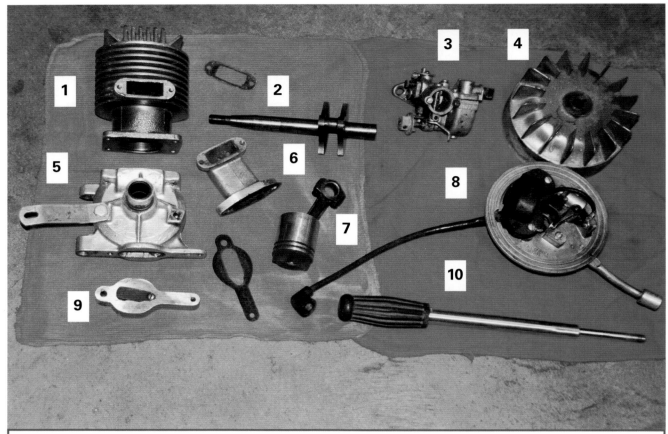

The "powerhead group" includes (1) air-cooled (finned) cylinder; (2) crankshaft; (3) Tillotson carburetor; (4) flywheel; (5) crankcase; (6) exhaust manifold; (7) piston and connecting-rod assembly; (8) magneto; (9) reed plate; (10) tiller; and assorted gaskets. All, except the magneto, flywheel, and carb are products of a tiny Southern California foundry.

This view shows the gearcase with the lower unit's skeg pan removed. A former owner added a grease fitting (not visible) to the side of the gearcase. The maker of this ultra-basic kicker simply recommended stuffing the lubrication into the gearbox while the pan was out of the way. That meant standing the whole motor up side down.

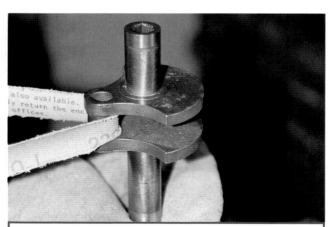

As is the case with many old motors, the Kit had been sitting in a damp place for a while. Consequently, the crankshaft sustained rust spots and a "stain" where the connecting rod gripped the crank throw. A thin strip of sandpaper and some back-and-forth action offered the cure.

The re-assembly gets underway, first with the transom clamp and torque tube . . . topped by the crankcase and crankshaft.

Assembly Instruction Manual he'd found in an antique shop. This gave the crew a fun chance to disassemble the Comanco and, using those six pages of step-by-step directions, build it up again, exactly as some long-forgotten boater had done with that very engine during the Eisenhower administration. We even tuned in the local oldies radio station and let Elvis set the shop mood.

Job one was a compression test, "Just to see if the tester's meter would even budge," a shop crewmember laughed. When the gauge screamed its way to 120 psi—readings almost double those recorded by the better-designed motors including our 1922 Johnson—everybody insisted on testing it a second and then a third time. The most accepted rationale theory on that 120-psi figure (originally anticipated to be in the 35- to 50-psi range) is that we simply had found "the lucky Comanco powerhead." While that's not a very scientific explanation, it does give credence to the reality that certain examples of inexpensively produced piston/cylinder mates happen to make a good match. However, not all was well with #8379:

• No spark.
• Scuffing and scratching on the piston.
• A worn connecting rod endcap.
• Wear evident on the piston wristpin.
• A worn crankshaft journal.
• Poor seating of the reed valve.
• Noise—like marbles grinding against one another—coming from the lower-unit gears.

After bathing the individual parts in solvent, drying them, wire-brushing for further cleanliness, and arranging the stuff on some shop rags, we decided to call this project a "modified fix-up." While the Kit was being subjected to a complete dismantling and cleaning, no attempt would be made to do anything other than get it running. Cosmetics were not an issue in this endeavor. The *Kit Outboard Motor Assembly Instruction Manual* claimed that one needed only the following tools and supplies to get underway:

6-inch adjustable wrench
4-inch screwdriver
10-inch screwdriver

The crankshaft and connecting rod are back in place and awaiting the endcap. This is a good example of a "plain-bearing" engine—there are no ball, roller, or needle bearings in the entire Kit. This design is typical of bargain-priced mills. Note how the imperfectly machined crankcase looks almost homemade.

A few twists of a hex wrench snug the endcap to the connecting rod.

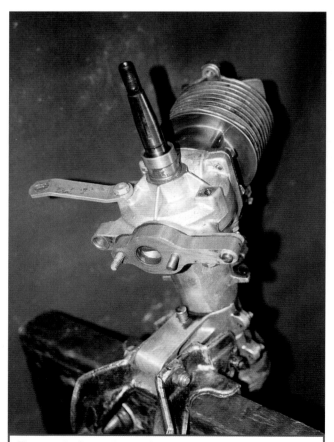

The cast-aluminum cylinder shined up nicely on the wire wheel. Lots of dirt was hiding between its cooling fins. The reed-valve "cage" is rejoined to the front of the crankcase.

The quality Tillotson carburetor mounts to the reed cage. In the Kit's original Miburn Cub incarnation, a proprietary or "no-name" carb was used. The reed "cage" also served as an adaptor for the better carburetor.

2 ounces of waterproof or outboard gear grease

1 ounce of Permatex gasket compound or shellac

A workbench on which a railing has been nailed to the front edge

Those without a workbench were directed to assemble their Kit outboard on a fence or chair back. We opted for a board secured by a vise, and felt free to use a wider variety of tools than the three recommended. Still, the rebuild took twice as long as suggested. Of course, closely inspecting the

With its fuel tank and rope sheave added, the Kit is complete. It sort of looks like the kind of funny little old outboard that the cartoon characters Alvin and the Chipmunks might use. Our subject motor's sputtering reminded the crew of an animated, sped-up voice soundtrack.

The do-it-yourself outboard concept was reprised in the late 1970s and early 1980s by the Mighty Mite folks. Theirs was also a single-cylinder putt-putt, but it was water-cooled and offered a bit more reliability.

decades-old parts and deciding on how those needing attention could be transformed into working order was not a consideration in 1958. The accompanying photos help tell the story. Not shown is the disappointment on the crew's faces when the completed Kit still refused to generate spark. So, off again came the fuel line, tank, rope sheave, and flywheel, a process repeated thrice until the fussy condenser was replaced, shorted wire discovered, and spark finally obtained.

The Kit's advantage over a more traditionally powered outboard is its air-cooling. Gassed up, it's ready to be tested in any well-ventilated place where neighbors won't object to a chainsaw-like sound. Ol' #8379 began sputtering on its fifth pull. Carburetor adjustments helped smooth it out somewhat, but after the dry-land test, nobody on the crew volunteered to take the little kicker away from the dock until a sturdy set of oars was stowed in the boat.

The magneto collar screw gets tightened around the crankcase shank, but not too tightly; otherwise, the spark-advance and spark-retard lever won't move.

RESTORATION CASE STUDIES

ALL IT NEEDS IS LOVE – 1964 MERCURY 39

At one end of Mercury's 1964 New York Boat Show display rested a cute, sparkling black and silver fishing motor. Dwarfing this single-cylinder kicker and stealing much of the fledgling's debut thunder, however, was the lineup's statuesque 100-horse, six-popper brother. As a 10-year-old, I immediately identified with the diminutive outboard and pulled my dad away from admiring those higher-powered mills long enough to suggest ordering one of the 3.9-horsepower Mercs for our rowboat.

"But, it only has one cylinder," he dismissed.

Several months later, my father presented me with a 6-horsepower Mercury Twin, a wonderful gift that still provides a great push and never gave us an ounce of trouble. Still, images of that lonely little Merc 39 at the end of the rack stayed with me. So, when (a coincidental 39 years later) *The Classic Outboard Motor Handbook* was being planned, I happily brought home a shopworn example spotted in a nautical flea market. Although cosmetically rather nicked-up, the reclining Merc felt like it had good compression "bounce" when its cord was slowly pulled. Its $100 price tag was about average for a mid-1960s, major-label "used, late model" motor with revitalization potential. On the drive home, though, I fully considered several common maladies that might reveal themselves upon a more precise inspection. After all, lower-unit seals, shift operability, carburetor condition, and fuel pump and water pump efficiency could not be taken for granted. Then there was the matter of not having had the opportunity to test-run that lucky little Merc 39 prior to carrying it to my waiting car.

Consulted for the planning phase was Pennsylvania Antique Outboard Motor Club member Bob Grubb, who has literally spent a lifetime around Mercs. His father founded one of Mercury's longest-operating dealerships, a business that, in the late 1980s, began specializing in vintage motors. Bob recommended I keep these Mercury Quicksilver replacement items on hand for the small motor's maintenance:

- Water pump impeller
- Ignition condenser
- Fuel pump diaphragm

While nearly 40 years old at the time of this writing, Merc 39 serial number 1701528 represented an era of low-power outboards still appearing on countless fresh waterways. (Engines used in saltwater tend to wear out much

The author with his Mercury 39. The 1964 single appeared to be in decent shape and hardly seemed to qualify as an antique outboard. Nevertheless, at press time, the little motor was in fact nearly 40 years old. That meant the engine had enough history to possess geriatric mechanical maladies.

sooner, due to the corrosive environment and its effects on water jackets, lower units, and other vital parts. They don't usually make satisfactory project motors.) When a customer requests a rough service estimate for a basic tune-up on an "old" kicker like the Merc 39, prices for the above components, sparkplugs, and the cost of shop labor would be tallied up for a minimum ballpark figure. However, because this would be a do-it-yourself deal, sans those labor charges, I felt free to add a can of touchup paint to the parts bill.

As the motor's examination began, one repair crewmember reported its little magneto delivering "a spark that'd give an August electrical storm stiff competition!"

With the hood removed, initial examination can be made. First to be asked: Are any parts missing? Nope, all accounted for. This example had even retained its tiny yellow plastic "keeper" caps over the three flywheel bolts. The fuel filter (cylindrical piece attached to the carburetor at the front of the powerhead) received a quick inspection and was found to be remarkably free of grit and dirt, indicating either a recent cleaning or overall good motor maintenance through the decades.

Deep paint gouges on the tiller hint at rough contact with a dock, boat, or car trunk. The light band around the handle a couple of inches from the base is melted rubber vibration cushioning that tends to quickly soften with even a season of sunlight exposure. For cosmetic purposes, this oozed area can be dressed up with an X-Acto knife and treated to touch-up paint.

Only a light coating of oily residue has adhered to a few surfaces of the Merc 39. No matter how slight, though, it must be cleaned from every nook and cranny. It's a fussy but important job in any thorough revitalization or restoration. Barely visible is the original Mercury "OK" inspection stamp above the cylinder head, signifying the motor was fit for shipment to a dealer.

Compression topped 100 psi and, with a quick twist of the red flywheel, bounced back via compression like a pinball zipping off a soft rubber bumper. Thanks to those successful signs and weather that was suddenly (for the first time in six months) bright and 80 degrees, I was reluctantly coaxed into clamping the still mostly mechanically mysterious Mercury on a handy 9-foot aluminum pram and giving it a go.

"But what if the fuel pump won't work or the water pump impeller is shot?" I asked the classic-outboarding instigators. They promised that an inoperable fuel diaphragm wouldn't cause further damage, as it'd simply prevent the Merc 39 from running. The impeller issue took a little more convincing because I had no interest in experiments potentially leading to a cooked piston or cylinder. In the end, the warm sunshine got the better of my "examine before you run it" judgment. I connected the remote fuel line, squeezed the primer bulb, made sure the gearshift lever was in neutral, twisted the tiller grip throttle/magneto control to start, activated the choke, looked back at the troublemakers on the dock, and pulled the starter cord.

The greasy coating on the lower unit could indicate leaky lower-unit seals or a cracked casting. Even on a relatively "modern" classic outboard, replacement seals are not always universally available. This might mean having to keep a suspicious eye on gear lube levels.

Degreasing exposes a suspicious imperfection. That's a bona fide crack in the lower-unit casting. Spent cooling water got trapped in there when the tiny weep-hole drain in the casting became blocked with dirt or some other debris from the lake. Some classic outboarders drill out these exits to make them more effective. Fortunately, this fissure isn't connected to the gearcase and its lube cavity. For the time being, the crew will just live with it.

No, team member Art DeKalb is not dipping that brush into a tub of black touch-up paint. The dark liquid is dirt and grease from the motor that mixed into the solvent used to clean the Merc 39.

The cleaned motor dries off in the rare north-central New York State March sun.

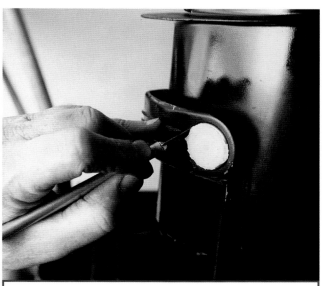

Prior to painting the lower unit, an emblem is masked off and the masking trimmed.

A gentle back-and-forth spray action about 12 inches from the surface (consult the directions on your paint can) starts making a big difference. Be careful to stop the spray only when it's not directed toward the target surface, otherwise paint "bunching" and "runs" can occur.

"Looks like a new motor," said a neighbor who dropped by to see the team's progress.

Remember me mentioning the 6-horsepower Merc I got as a kid? The engine's always-dependable performance prevented me from getting much experience troubleshooting and fixing motors like it. Now, my hands-on education under the hood of a similar-vintage Mercury would have to remain on hold, as the 3.9 single responded busily to that first pull. Obviously fuel was pulsing to its carburetor. Water streamed from the telltale as if it had dreams of helping extinguish a five-alarm fire.

So, what does one decide to do for a "relatively old" outboard, such as the Merc 39, that shows few geriatric symptoms? This case led me to clean it, use the touchup paint, and pencil an appointment on the shop calendar for a winter's afternoon water impeller and fuel pump diaphragm replacement. And, there's the matter of a lower-unit crack that became visible in the sheen of a fresh coat of black enamel. Good precautions include checking the gearcase lube level regularly and not storing the motor in a place where water that's trapped in the cooling system and lower unit can freeze and crack things. Otherwise, treating as an old friend any classic motor you enjoy running is a good prescription: Be sensitive to things that truly need attention and know what to save for a leisurely winter afternoon in your basement outboard shop.

When this photo was snapped, the hood was still a few days away from having its original decal (replacements are tough to find) masked and given a shiny black touch-up coat.

The gearcase required very little lube before good, clean oil began exiting from the upper-vent screw hole, indicating that the gearbox must have been recently filled. None was observed exiting the aforementioned crack area.

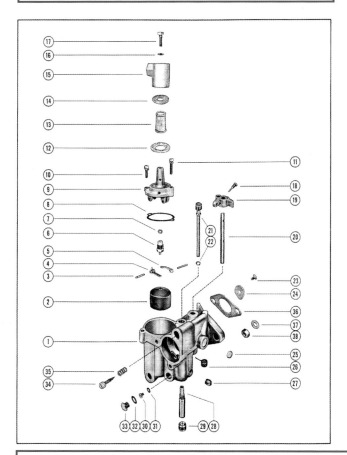

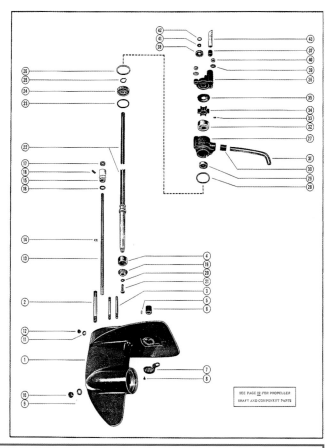

These Mercury parts sheets show a Tillotson carburetor, with its user-serviceable fuel-filter assembly at the top, and the lower-unit assembly with an exploded view of the water pump at the upper right.

Back to the Shop: The Importance of Crankcase Compression

Shortly before *The Classic Outboard Motor Handbook* went to press, I decided to take some friends for a ride up the Oswego River branch of the Erie Canal. For power, I chose the nice-running Merc 39. This time out, though, it wouldn't pump sufficient cooling water, nor would it stay running on any setting below "fast."

Truth be told, it's not uncommon for an old kicker, especially one that hasn't recently been "gone through" in the shop, to develop problems, seemingly suddenly and for no logical reason. But there's always a root cause. In this case, the original pump impeller had given up the ghost and a new impeller did the trick. The poor-to-non-functioning idle, however, was a real puzzler. No matter how we adjusted the carburetion, it ran too lean (less fuel than air in the mixture) and died unless choked every few seconds. After several hours of troubleshooting, we discovered low crankcase compression.

While cylinder compression is vital, pressure on the intake, or crankcase, side of the engine is crucial, too. Without it, the proper fuel/air mixture isn't passed along to the cylinder. A simple test to determine the presence of crankcase compression is to remove the carburetor and lay a tissue or other sensitive membrane over the opening on the crankcase. If, when you pull the starter cord, the tissue wiggles, it indicates at least some compression. Curiously, in the case of the Merc 39, we discovered that either someone had not tightened the screws designed to secure the top main-bearing crankcase seal to the crankcase, or they had vibrated loose. Correcting this basic error helped the situation, but new crankcase seals (top and bottom) were recommended for the motor's anticipated winter maintenance.

The new impeller slides down the driveshaft to the pump body. Before jockeying it into its tiny keyway, the mechanic should put a bit of grease on the vanes to facilitate insertion. Note the rust-pitted driveshaft, indicating water was trapped in the area over a period of time. It looks ugly, but can be tolerated.

Master Mercury mechanic Bob Grubb is satisfied that the motor is nicely pumping water, but when a variety of carburetor adjustments don't yield results, he suspects poor crankcase compression. Art DeKalb listens for fuel/air mixture–related symptoms.

Either a previous mechanic failed to tighten the top crankcase screws, or they vibrated loose. Securing them improved crankcase compression to an acceptable level, but new crankcase seals were prescribed.

Now pumping ample cooling water and with much of its crankcase compression restored, our Merc 39 happily leaves a New York State Canal System buoy in its wake. It still had problems running smoothly below "shift range" or fast idle, but seemed to best love being mated to its 9-foot 1962 Arkansas Traveler aluminum pram and trying to chase the neighbors' personal watercraft.

RESTORATION CASE STUDIES

COAXING KICK FROM A QUIET TROLLER—1950s MINN-KOTA ELECTRIC

By the mid-1980s, vintage electric trolling motors were trickling into Antique Outboard Motor Club swap meets. Electrics such as the 1895 Allen Electric Oar and the 1900 Submerged Electric were among the first outboards, but examples of classic post–World War II, battery-powered kickers have traditionally enjoyed only modest support among old-outboard enthusiasts. This small following being a key ingredient in supply-and-demand economics, the thousands of these vintage trollers seen in garage sales, estate auctions, and "penny-saver" papers can be acquired very reasonably. A pair of $25 classic Minn-Kota trolling motors was purchased by a *Classic Outboard Handbook* repair team member to add what he laughed would be "a *shocking* dimension to vintage marine propulsion literature."

Selected for examination was a model *TS* Minn-Kota, serial number 4429. Although it had areas of surface rust, as well as splotches of dried-up oil stuck with dust and sand, this troller's propeller could be freely spun, in turn demonstrating that the electric motor possessed promise. The unit's questionably ratty leads were touched to a handy lawn tractor battery, causing the prop to begin moving in a palsied fashion. A snappy spark from the powerhead ended the direct experimentation, and gave credence to our original assumption that those key wires were frayed bare at the grommet in the motor cover.

On the workbench stand the Minn-Kota project began by following the "dismantle and clean-up" procedure identical to that used on our gas motors. Admittedly, though, having never worked on an electric troller, we were flying blind in its deconstruction. A period service bulletin would have been a wise addition to the shop clipboard. Happily one was found, but not until the second session of the project. Before this, several likely screws were removed so that the powerhead cover could be taken off. These did nothing to loosen the piece, so more were unscrewed, eventually enabling the powerhead cover's crown to be dethroned. Immediately, source of that sand/dirt was evident: mud daubers! These insects are a menace to classic outboarders, because they can get into almost any opening and then fill it with an often-corrosive mud nest. Conditions in a gas engine's parts (like the carburetor) are even more susceptible to mud dauber damage, because any

One team member predicted the Minn-Kota would be "$25 worth of trouble," but that didn't turn out to be the case. In fact, this old electric motor made for a nice project that later played a role in an equally enjoyable fishing trip.

foreign matter pulled into the crankcase can score the crankshaft, pistons, and cylinder, in addition to clogging fuel passages. This mud in a water inlet or other portion of the cooling system may lead to a motor fatality. So there's another plus for outboards like the old Minn-Kota: It is free from many of the mechanical systems that can trouble its gasoline-powered sisters.

Once the powerhead was disconnected from the drive-shaft housing, the fine condition of the lower bearing (holding the armature shaft) could be noted. It allowed the

Name, rank, and serial number. After checking the maker's records, it appears this tag was originally affixed by a Minn-Kota factory worker in 1956.

The bronze top—main bearing appears to be in good shape, despite some rust and stuck screws. Most well-built objects from the "old days" were meant to be taken apart for servicing, giving even stubborn fasteners reasonable potential for cooperation with a serious screwdriver or wrench. If you're using propane torch heat as a "convincer," don't be overzealous and inadvertently melt or de-solder wire connections!

Popping the hood reveals some pretty dusty wiring. Of course, dusty is better than burnt, tampered-with, or corroded, so things don't look to be hopeless.

The powerhead was easily removed from the torque tube, but until an ancient Minn-Kota parts book came our way, we couldn't figure out how to extract the armature. Finding those factory-encrypted directions for navigating disassembly the "right way" made us feel like secret code breakers.

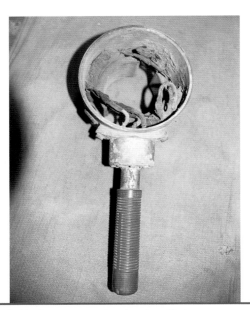

A view inside the center armature housing still shows some mud residue, even after an initial cleaning.

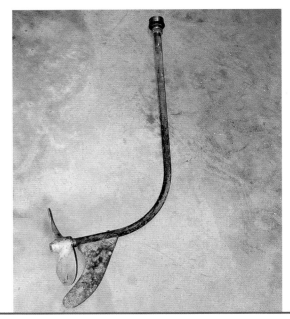

Discretion was the better part of valor when deciding whether or not to remove the flexible "speedometer cable" driveshaft from the torque tube. We opted to bypass this puzzler, but refilled the tube with oil.

Light sanding freshens up the armature contact areas. Experimenting with different sandpaper grits, from fine to medium, is the best way to find a cure without inflicting further damage. Be careful not to bear down or stroke unevenly on the sandpaper, otherwise you'll create an uneven surface.

"Just plain old rusty, muddy crud" was the best terminology the team could come up with to describe what was hiding in the Minn-Kota's darkest recesses. This is a view of one of the transom bracket/motor swivel halves.

armature shaft to spin like a well-balanced top. Try as we might, though, we could not get the bearing out of its seat in the powerhead/armature's lower cover or "bottom bell." Neither would the propeller screw that held the prop onto the flexible driveshaft cable break loose. The flexible shaft, like an automotive speedometer cable, reacted in perpetual recoil when this prop screw was turned. Both situations demanded a decision common to all puzzling roadblocks in classic-outboard repair: Do you stop until a better idea or more information becomes available, keep attempting to unscrew the assumed correct connectors and risk causing some damage, or simply work around the offending area?

Waiting for a better understanding of the old Minn-Kota's proprietary construction turned out to be the wisest way to proceed, albeit frustrating at the time. On the commute home from the outboard shop, I had vague junior high–era memories of having sent off to several electric outboard makers for "any old catalogs or manuals."

A can of "hammered" finish spray paint is shown with the Minn-Kota's repainted bell housing. This touch represents a bit of artistic license, as the troller was originally a single color.

The electric troller's top hat cleans up nicely after being "hammertoned."

The center armature housing and tiller received fresh paint. Note that the grip was masked to prevent over-spray. Most buffs believe that cosmetic parts in serviceable condition (at least a 6 on a scale of 1 to 10) should be preserved instead of replaced. While few casual observers would scrutinize the presence of an adapted bicycle handlebar grip, most boat-show judges appreciate recognizable original equipment.

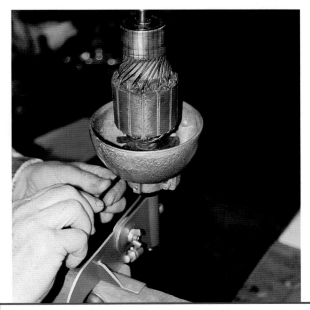

Getting it together. The restored armature and bell housing are secured to the torque tube.

Wedged in a dog-eared manila file folder in my office was a circa 1960 Minn-Kota parts list and instructions sheet. What a revelation to see that it included just what a motor doctor would order: a section titled "Reconditioning Troller." We followed the yellowed paper with great success, reading:

- Clamp the troller to something solid.
- Remove the two Tie Bolts (#248). To assure no damage to heads, use proper size screwdriver.

- Remove Motor Cap (#252). This can be pried off by inserting screwdriver in air gap between the Cap and the Field Ring Housing (#251).
- Loosen brush wires and lift Brush Holder (#235) by tapping lightly.
- Lift the entire Field Ring Housing, including the contents (field coil assembly, etc.) from the Bottom Bell (#238/238-D).
- Remove the motor from the Main Drive Tube (#207) by loosening and removing the two Hollow Head Cap

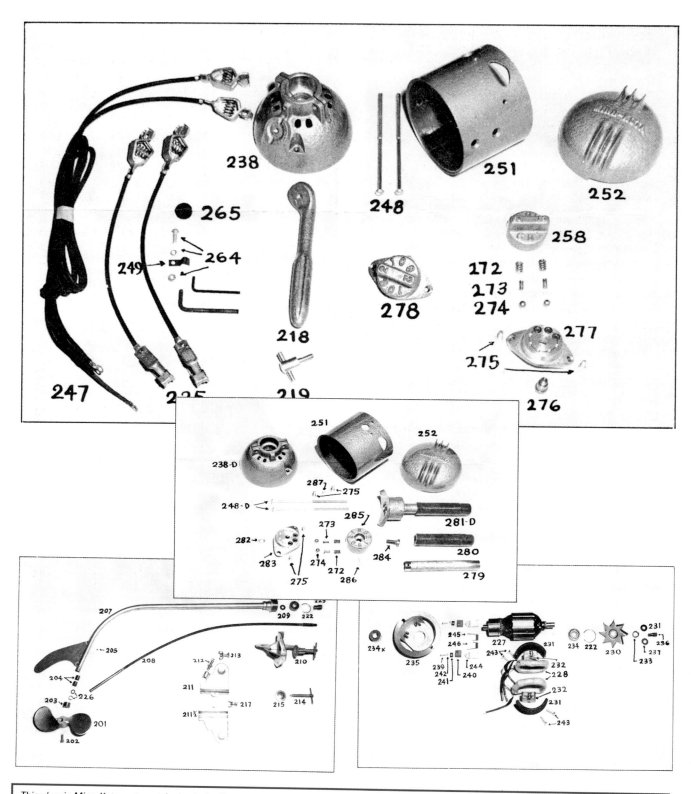

This classic Minn-Kota parts cataloging helps illustrate the directions in our text. Whenever available, such parts references should be acquired and studied. They usually make a revitalization or restoration much easier than flying blind.

Screws (#250) and the Hollow Head Set Screw with an Allen wrench.

• Remove Hexdrive (#236) and washer, which will now enable you to lift the Armature (#227) from the Bottom Bell.

• Remove Fan (#230), Spacer (#233), and Washer (#229).

You are now ready to proceed with whatever repair is necessary. When turning the commutator, be sure it is perfectly smooth. Don not undercut. If you need to replace the bearing in the Bottom Bell, remove Lock Ring (#222) and bearing will come out.

In fact, removal of that aforementioned "lock ring" did the trick. From there, we were able to clean and service (by light sanding and a few instances of replacing frayed wiring) the armature. As soon as the following official Minn-Kota directions were observed, the flexible driveshaft (or cable) seemed to have changed its mind about being uncooperative:

• Remove cable locating screw (#220) from rear of adapter.

• Place 1/8-inch pin in hole in cable left by the removal of the screw. Remove socket drive (#223) from top of adapter with 3/8-inch hex wrench.

• Remove 1/8-inch pin and loosen packing nut (#203) located directly behind propeller. Slide cable out of cable shaft and replace with new cable.

Our classic Minn-Kota's driveshaft cable looked pretty good, so it simply got cleaned, re-greased by "removal of the small greasing plug screw (#205) located about 4 inches back from the propeller, and forcing in any good outboard motor grease." Minn-Kota said the lack of grease would lead to an "irritating rattle-like noise" but cause "no harm." The company suggested owners might "place a few drops of good oil on the upper motor bearing (#234) and on the upper bearing in the main drive tube."

An electric troller such as the ubiquitous Minn-Kota (and their clones including the Pioneer) makes for a unique classic-outboard project. Other old-line makes with above-water powerheads such as LeJay also offer a neat way to toot around some quiet waterway in vintage style. Cosmetics on these kickers typically consist of some paint and possibly a small decal. Some, such as the subject Minn-Kota wore its brand cast into the aluminum powerhead cover. That's always a durable visual plus.

By the way, while there's no fuel mixture to follow, juice is an issue. Old trollers like our Minn-Kota were built in a 6-volt auto battery world. The company promised super performance when two 6-volt batteries were hooked up in series to generate 12-volts. Even for 6-volt operation, Minn-Kota suggested a pair of car batteries wired in parallel to increase trolling time between necessary battery charges. Anyone who tries toting a couple of *Happy Days*–era auto

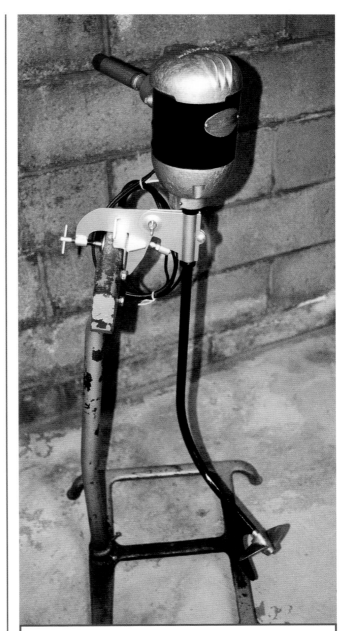

Ready to troll again! The fish won't know that this little motor is actually an ancient mariner, and even the most curious admirer shouldn't have reason to suspect it was recently a $25 junker.

batteries from the boat to the garage for charging knows why vintage electric outboards were considered to be second-best when compared to a small gas-powered kicker. We've discovered, however, that one of classic outboarding's best kept secrets is the low-maintenance fun you can enjoy with a fixed-up, revitalized, or restored old electric troller and an ultra-efficient, modern deep-cycle marine battery.

CHAPTER 6
KEEP YOUR CLASSIC KICKER RUNNING NICELY

At one time, I squeezed about 150 old outboards into the very small basement of my home. Some major league classic kicker buffs have collections that'd make any grouping of less than 200 vintage motors look meager, but please stay with the image of a hundred and a half engines in the very small basement of my first house.

Everyone "treated" to a tour would descend only three or four stairs before exclaiming something like, "Oh my gosh! I've never seen so many outboards!" While collectors get a proud chuckle out of such reactions, they're usually nonplused by the visitor's inevitable next question, a query that seems quite logical to the uninformed: "Do they *all* run?" In most cases, the answer is no, although each enthusiast's huge outboard harem is likely to include several prized engines that get the royal treatment and are always ready to go. Even the collector with only a half-dozen kickers has a couple of tried-and-true machines in that lot. Typically, they wear a paper tag or note card briefly chronicling when the motor was last used, its best carb settings, when it was most recently greased, and a sentence or two about its idiosyncrasies. If you're like most people, you are mighty glad the car repair place puts a little sticker on your windshield to remind you when the vehicle's oil needs changing. Imagine the value that these simple memory joggers on your vintage outboards can provide. With just a glance, you'll have reference to any kicker's vital stats, especially its optimum fuel mixture diet.

MODERN OIL AND GAS FOR VINTAGE MOTORS

Comedian Jackie Mason got big laughs with a routine about how his mother always cajoled him to consume more of the delicious roast beef she'd prepared. "Every time I sat at the table she begged, 'Eat! Eat!' Then I hear some medical report on the radio about how meat can give you a heart attack. For years, I thought my mother loved me," Mason cried, "but I find out she was trying to kill me!"

Anyone aggravated by contradictory medical findings that prove, at least until the next report, that something is either good or bad for you, should be able to identify with the controversy over which oil is safest for old two-cycle outboards. It's best to begin by suggesting that the answer probably depends on whom you ask. Also at issue is the query of how old the particular vintage mill actually is. You'll need to know its predominant type of engine bearings: bronze or the more sophisticated needle or roller styles. As a generalization, the latter kinds of bearings (also known as "full-jeweled," a term started by sophisticated watchmakers and borrowed circa 1947 as a marketing status symbol by Mercury), require less oil in the fuel mixture because they are subject to less friction than are stationary bronze bushings and bearings.

Regardless of the specific powerhead components, however, every motor needs adequate lubrication. Skimping on a few ounces of oil can cause big problems. I've long been a student of the imaginary Institute for Advanced Conservative Studies on Outboard Friction Concerns, which teaches

Because they're properly maintained and operated, any one of these "experienced" outboards would make a positive impression on people seeing and hearing them in action. This is true whether the motors are teamed with classic hulls or clamped to the stern of a garden-variety aluminum rowboat. In fact, contemporary boaters and personal watercraft riders alike slowed to give an admiring look as this riverfront scene was assembled.

Kicker Tips 6.1
Tag Every Motor You Bag

It only takes two motors to constitute a collection. Whether one of a pair or part of a menagerie several dozen strong, each of your vintage outboards will benefit from being tagged with its vital statistics. This info can easily be noted on a 3x5 index card and consulted for service schedules or historical detail. Here's a useful motor tag template:

Make_____ Year_____ Model_____ Serial #_____

Purchase date_____ From_____ Price: $_____

Problem aspects:

Parts needed:

Motor to be/Motor is: _____(Parted Out) _____(Fixed-Up) _____(Revitalized) _____(Restored)

Date of last run_____ Performance:

Fuel mix ratio: Best needle valve settings:

Service record:

It's not uncommon for the basement of a classic-outboard collector to get so filled with motors that one's eyes have to adjust to the mish-mash of aluminum, brass, and steel just to find a particular engine within the crowd. Anyone who stocked a cellar like this knows the importance of making sure that any leaky gearcase has a pie plate under it and all of the fuel tanks, carburetors, and fuel lines have been drained. Important, too, is that the motor storage area be dry. A dehumidifier helps greatly in moisture-prone environments, especially during the summer.

Here's how a vintage outboard collection often begins: one kid, one favorite old motor, and then—years later—the chance to recapture great memories by buying an antique engine (or two, or three) just like it.

it's better to go a little "fat" on oil. In other words, some of us traditionally view a smoky blue exhaust as a sign of adequate oil in the gas. Lately, though, I have begun coursework in other schools of marine-lubrication thought (See Kicker Tip 6.3). The variety of choices doesn't make a novice classic-outboard buff's oil selection process easy. In fact, even some longtime members of The Antique Outboard Motor Club have been confused by the robust "best oil" debate that tends to yield convincing arguments from almost every side.

It would seem that a classic motor's original owner's manual would shed light on the subject. But, the instruction booklet for a 1952 Evinrude model 3012 Lightwin, for example, only offers more variables: "We recommend *Mobiloil Outboard* or another outboard oil, or a regular SAE 30 grade automotive engine oil." While the manual verifies that a major motor manufacturer sanctioned standard car oil, as well as the then rather new two-cycle outboard lubricants, it's logical to assume Evinrude would have embraced natural TC-W and synthetics (with TC-W specs) had these oils been available in

The *Best* Needle Valve Setting: Hard to Pin Down

Back in the 1930s, Evinrude used to tag its outboards' carburetor needle valves with a little brass medallion. The writing on the little disc included a miniscule stamping that revealed that particular motor's optimum needle valve setting. Most either said a one-half or three-quarters turn from closed when starting the motor cold. That's a good trial and error starting point for any vintage outboard. However, once the engines gets going, the needle valve setting will likely need further attention.

Old kickers often had prominent needle valve control knobs because, just like in the early days of radio and TV sets, adjusting things was part of the routine. Be advised that lots of small vintage outboards have only one needle valve (used for regulating fuel flow, whether *rich* or *lean,* into the carburetor), while bigger or more sophisticated motors also possess a low-speed adjustment. Because the *start* position is well advanced past *slow*, the high-speed needle valve is the one that's active. Experimenting to find your classic's needle valve "sweet spot" is part of the fun of vintage outboarding. Just don't tighten down the valve too hard, as it'll damage the valve seat.

Classic Outboard Motor Handbook shop team member Art DeKalb offers further details on pinning down those needle valve settings. For 1950s OMC varieties (Evinrude, Johnson, and Gale Products) in any horsepower denomination, open the high-speed knob three-quarters to one turn to get underway. The low-speed needle valve should be closed to about one-half turn for the cold start. It's best to run on a boat (as opposed to unventilated test tank) so the motor does not eat its own exhaust, which causes very poor running. When running, adjust high-speed to fastest boat speed and then, after throttling down the motor to *slow,* open low-speed one-half turn and continue slowing the motor, while adjusting the low-speed needle for a good (trolling) idle. That should provide good settings for later operation.

For fishing-size motors from the 1930s, dial the needle valve open one-half to three-quarters turn. Adjust for the best speed and smoothest operation, as above.

If the motor coughs, the mixture is lean. Open the needle valve a little, and try again. If no firing occurs, take a sparkplug out and see if its electrode area is wet or dry. If the plug is wet (with fuel), dry it off and close the needle some. If the sparkplug is dry, open the needle. If after several pulls there's still no success, check the plugs again. A teaspoon of gas squirted in the sparkplug hole sometimes helps.

As for "generic" and "average" settings, they don't work on every outboard. Many motors *will not start or run* if the needle is one-eighth turn off its correct setting—and settings are different for different motors. Some motors want to be choked a lot to get going, while some flood easily and don't respond well to being choked. It's best to listen to the motor *tell* you whether it is too rich or too lean. Little 1930s motors like their needle valves to get a one-half turn from closed . . . approximately. Truth is, though, each motor has a *personality* and loves particular needle valve settings. That's why its owner needs to become familiar with his or her particular classic kicker.

Finally, for 1930s and 1940s Johnson models LT, DT, AT, and, TD/TN that sometimes show up for sale, there is a little auxiliary needle setting to deal with, too. Begin with three-quarters turn open and once the idle is set with that needle (feel and listen for smooth operation), leave it at this optimum position.

the early 1950s. In fact, the same manual warns Lightwin owners to "use metal containers only" for mixing and toting fuel. Few would argue that this means today's ubiquitous red plastic gas cans could prove harmful to classic Evinrudes.

Something original equipment fuel instructions can be counted on for, though, is the fuel mixture ratio. If a 1950s outboard was supposed to take 1/2 pint of oil per gallon (or 16:1) of gasoline, it's safe to follow that directive now, even if you're using a TC-W3 oil that says it's a 50:1. Even though there are knowledgeable vintage outboarders who run engines as old as World War I–era rowboat motors on only 1/4 pint per gallon of gas (32:1) using synthetic oil, for purposes of just getting started in the hobby, it's best to use the original suggested mixture. Whatever oil you choose, be sure it isn't marked "diluted" or "pre-diluted." It's best to know the motor will be fed the "straight" stuff as opposed to oil that's been cut with some unknown substance unfriendly to elderly engine parts.

A colorful display of just some of the hundreds of outboard oil brands offered from the 1940s onward. Most are of the 1950s two-cycle or "outboard" type. While some buffs covet this thick, vintage black gold for their classic outboards, most agree that modern TC-W3 outboard oil used in accordance with the motor maker's gas/oil mixture specifications is the best way to go.

This motor is running in the test tank just after having been rebuilt. Consequently, it has extra oil in its fuel mix for break-in purposes—and smoking as a result. Under normal conditions, it shouldn't be such a belcher.

Kicker Tips 6.3

Schools of Marine-Lubrication Thought

• **Standard (non-detergent) SAE 30 automotive oil.** This lube was primarily designed for a four-cycle automotive engine crankcase. Because the consumption of oil is not in a car's best interest, this thick stuff (as compared to the lighter consistency of modern outboard oil) wasn't meant to burn. Nor was it formulated to mix well with gasoline.

• **1950s-style two-cycle engine oil.** Classic-outboard buffs have called this "black gold" and seek stock cans of it at every old marina and gas station they encounter. It's thick like automotive oil, but was concocted to stay better mixed with gas and to burn more efficiently than garden-variety automotive lubricant.

• **TC-W petroleum-based.** The letters stand for **T**wo **C**ycle, **W**ater-cooled and are typically followed by a numeral (1, 2, or 3) indicating the lubricant technology is still evolving; series 3 is current as of this writing. TC-W oil differs from the first-generation two-cycle stuff described above that one would use in outboards and air-cooled equipment such as chainsaws or two-stroke lawnmowers (once a staple of the low-end power mower market). Generally, it is thinner than automotive and early two-stroke engine oils.

• **Synthetic outboard oil (with TC-W rating).** While not all varieties are natural petroleum-based products, synthetic, two-cycle outboard oil has a reputation for being the "oiliest" lube ever. That is to say, it has a reputation for reaching, coating, and sticking to all of a powerhead's moving parts. Additionally, it doesn't break down or thin out in extreme engine temperatures. This allows slightly higher than normal rpm and horsepower. Some proponents indicate that such slippery tenacity allows for using significantly less oil in each gallon of gasoline than would be the case with "the real thing." This is likely due to synthetics eventually passing through the engine as opposed to being burned in the combustion chamber. Happy results include an absence of carbon build-up in the cylinder, and piston rings that can be flexible enough to increase compression.

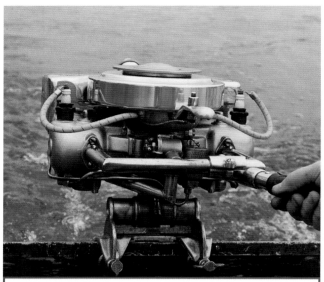

This antique outboard is operating on a clean-burning mix of modern, lead-free regular gas and synthetic TC-W3 outboard oil. Not a puff of smoke in sight. For larger classics, some might use a mid-range, 89-octane gasoline.

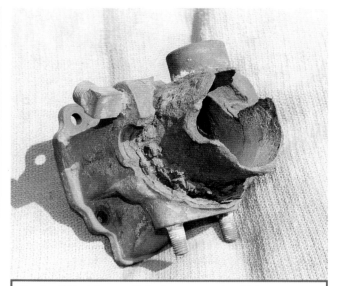

Here's a 1930s Johnson cylinder from a motor that didn't get cooling water properly drained from its water jacket. It's an extreme case, but not unheard of in antique-outboard circles. Rust eventually ate through the cylinder.

Good oil versus bad lube. Comparison photos from a 1960 Valvoline outboard oil pamphlet tell the story. "Wear and varnish formation are minimized on the piston on the left," noted the brochure, because it was protected with clean-burning oil. "Look for bright spots on these two pistons," it suggested. "The bright spots on the piston on the left are actually bare metal surfaces, which reveal the low deposit-forming tendencies" of a quality outboard oil. Finally, the ad piece noted, plug deposits and fouling on the right-hand sparkplug come from oil that doesn't burn well. Sparkplugs can be a good indicator of an engine's health.

Many old plugs can be cleaned and reused. Here, one of late-1940s vintage is wire-brushed. If revitalizing a sparkplug, be certain not to get dirt, wire hairs, or anything else microscopic stuck in the electrode end of the plug—it might later dislodge into the motor's combustion chamber and cause damage.

Retired commercial airline pilot and active vintage outboard restorer and operator Bill Salisbury tries many types of oil in his engines, and then takes them apart to compare the microscopic wear sustained with each given lubricant. The lion's share of his mills are 1930s racing outboards that demand a strict fuel mixture. Here, Salisbury comments on the use of various lubes and indicates why he's shifted some of his motors to newer oil technology:

Synthetics do burn to some extent, but tend not to burn as much as petroleum-based types. When they do burn, they smoke just like petroleum-based oils. The synthetics have a much higher resistance to scorching or "coking" and because of that, the carbon that they do produce when burning will not cause piston rings to stick in the grooves nor will the under-sides of the pistons become coked up with heavy carbon. The same applies to the carbon build-up at

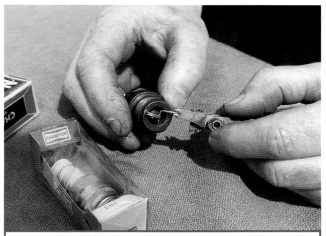

A feeler gauge is used to gap a sparkplug to the outboard maker's specifications. While new old-stock plugs that match the motor manufacturer's original recommendations can still be hunted down, contemporary sparkplugs can be used successfully when their heat range specs (and sometimes original numbers) are cross-matched via a current plug catalog or chart. A knowledgeable auto parts customer-service rep should be able to help.

You're looking at a slip of heavy white paper stuck between an old outboard's ignition points. Sometimes quickly moving a little piece of cardstock a few times through the point contacts will remove the dirt, corrosion, or rust spots that prevented the magneto from firing.

the exhaust ports. Simply put, the synthetics can withstand much higher temperatures before trouble starts. The "raw" oil that does go out of the ports is minimized because of the much thinner ratios required for good lubrication. What raw oil does go into the water is oftentimes a biodegradable.

As far as the use of automotive non-detergent oil, that's no longer necessarily a good lube to use in old outboards, even though it was written up as a recommendation in many of the original instruction manuals. Auto oil has low resistance to high heat and will scorch and clog cylinder ports and stick piston rings. If a person feels he or she must use an old-fashioned petroleum oil, one that I have found to work very well is a single viscosity ashless dispersant aviation oil (but not the aviation straight mineral oil). These oils are available in 30, 40, and 50 weights. Aeroshell W80 is a 40 weight, W100 is a 50 weight. The ashless dispersant quality keeps the oil from scorching and does seem to keep rings and ports clean.

I prefer to use this type of oil in old racing engines and usually mix it at a ratio of one quart per gallon (4:1) for racing engines such as Elto/Evinrude 4-60 or Johnson model SR or PR that run at 6,000 rpm or more. This oil will also run just fine in a stock model PO Johnson at 16:1.

The old type of two-cycle or "outboard" oils work fine in most of the old engines, and I recommend that the original ratio be maintained when using this type.

The "telltale" water stream several inches below the "R" in the Mercury name announces a nicely operating cooling system. Additional water and a bit of exhaust is "spritzing" from an auxiliary discharge nozzle farther back.

A tube of outboard lube is fitted with a grease gun–type nozzle. This lubricant is formulated for use on throttle and shift linkage areas.

Typically, non-shift motors are treated with grease, while shift models use a less viscous lube. Most buffs agree that Lubriplate 105 is well suited for non-shift classics. There are a couple of varieties of 105, so make sure the label says it's for outboards.

TC-W3 oils can be used in a more sparing ratio in some cases, but care must be exercised to use the recommended ratio with engines that have all plain bearings. Plain bearings like oil, and plenty of it. Roller bearings, on the other hand, run just fine on a much thinner mix. An all-roller-bearing engine runs fine on 50:1 using TC-W3 oil.

Synthetics can often be cut to a finer ratio, but I can only speak for AMSOIL, since it is the only one I've ever used. I settled on using a 32:1 ratio with AMSOIL for all my plain-bearing engines. On the all-roller-bearing engines, I use 64:1, or 2 ounces per gallon, which works very well. In fact, I have run my Johnson 1930 model VR-50 dual-carb racing engine at 24:1 using AMSOIL synthetic.

For most classic outboarders with a collection of standard-service motors, garden-variety TC-W3 oil should be fine if, as Salisbury notes, it's mixed with gasoline in the ratio originally specified by the outboard factory.

The instruction brochure for my 1965 Mercury 6-horsepower twin stated, "A good grade of marine white gasoline should be used." Back then, Amoco high test was about the only "white," or lead-free, gas. The local Merc dealer was also an Amoco station, but my dad hated to spend the exorbitant price of 36 cents a gallon for the stuff. If I weren't there to make a fuss, he would lug home a tank of leaded regular grade gas. This always made me feel as if I were feeding spoiled milk to some starving child, and it was difficult to have to admit that the outboard seemed to run better on the cheap stuff.

By 1980, leaded fuels were on their way out and octane ratings were reclassified in such a reduction of nomenclature that the old Amoco 100-octane gas might have been considered on a par with jet fuel! Although most manufacturers of now-classic outboards didn't preach high-test (that 1952 Evinrude manual stated, "High octane or highly leaded gas gives no advantage"), they might have taken some issue with the relatively low-octane (87) lead-free gasoline now commonplace. All of this narrative is an introduction to my nonscientific belief that one may obtain good results with a mid-range (89 octane) gas. I prize a 1954 Martin 200 that had a distressing knock or clunk at low to moderate speeds. At an Antique Outboard Motor Club meet, someone heard the noise, wagged his finger at me, and admonished, "Shame on you. You're using that cheap regular gas!" The guy predicted the big Martin would be happier on 89 octane, and he was right. That's why I typically feed my classic mills their manufacturer's originally recommended fuel mixture (often it's 1/2 pint to the gallon) using a synthetic TC-W3 oil and mid-grade gasoline. For most of these old timers, that's probably equivalent to a delicious roast beef dinner. Of course many classic outboarders continue to have good luck on convenience-store brand regular gas and TC-W3 oil wearing some discount-mart label. Watch out for gas that's heavily treated with additives to satisfy area-specific environmental regulations. A local mechanic who has worked on engines run with this stuff should be able to give you information about its side effects on small engines. That's part of the hobby's ongoing fun—being open to a little experimentation and using the mix that your old mill seems to like best.

IN-SEASON MAINTENANCE

Old-time kickers are fun to run because they require an admirable level of devotion. Not just anybody has the personality to intuitively understand his or her machine. For example, as soon as one's kicker starts, he or she must vigilantly ask, "Is it pumping water?" Most vintage motors have telltale water outlets that allow final inspection of this vital cooling function. There are times when poor flow or the complete void of a water stream is simply the province of a plugged outlet. When that's the case, a piece of wire or straightened paperclip can take care of a shallow blockage. Occasionally, something other than water gets sucked into the water intake, water lines, or water jackets, causing a stoppage that requires disassembly and cleaning. Insects and small critters have been known to deposit stuff in water intakes (and exhausts). Often, though, the water pump is the culprit, requiring a new impeller, wobble agitator, or freed-up action of the plunger, depending on its type. Because a water-cooled outboard deprived of water can get problematically hot within minutes, monitoring the motor's telltale (if so equipped) is an extremely useful visual maintenance.

Without becoming compulsive or paranoid, other things about your running classic to be sensitive to, include:

- **Flywheel tightly secured to the crankshaft.** Some vintage outboards, such as the 1928–1931 Elto Speedster, tend to loosen their flywheel nut. On motors with exposed flywheels it is especially easy to be sure it's tight. Yes, flywheels have been known to fly off the motor and cause injury to engine, boat, or driver.
- **Lower unit lubrication and condition of seals.** Grease around the gearcase could signal a leaky seal. And, if grease or gearcase oil is escaping, water usually enters to fill the void and rust the gears. Prepare to replace seals during the off-season. Meanwhile, keep the gearcase filled with lubricant.
- **Transom clamps tight and a safety chain hooked to motor.** Scuba divers don't like this advice, but a surprising number of outboards have popped off the boat for lack of tightened thumbscrews. Older, opposed-cylinder motors, especially, are quite capable of vibrating themselves loose. It's also good to take a precautionary wrench or screwdriver to these mills several times per season. Chances are a screw or bolt will need some re-tightening.
- **Sparkplug condition.** The gap should fulfill the motor maker's recommendation, and the plug needs to be free of dirt and carbon. When cleaning existing plugs, make certain to scrape or blow out all grit particles so that none can drop off into the cylinder and scratch up the works. Sparkplug companies suggest installing new plugs primarily for this reason.

Kicker Tips 6.4

For Every Month in Winter Season, Turn, Turn, Turn

One of the easiest ways to be assured that the old mills in your collection aren't getting rusted up inside is by making the rounds from flywheel to flywheel (or starter cord). Having stored those motors with a squirt of oil through the sparkplug hole in each cylinder, and rotated the flywheel, make it a monthly practice to slowly turn each flywheel a revolution or two. That way you'll keep current on the general condition of the individual outboards in the menagerie.

Some say it's best to park the flywheel's rotation at just the point where compression begins, so the exhaust ports are covered. More than a few buffs have expressed shock at discovering that a favorite motor (sometimes a restored one) became rust "stuck" from having remained motionless for a few years. Disappointing, too, is finding too late that a mouse nest that has corroded the carb, muffler, exhaust ports, or some other part.

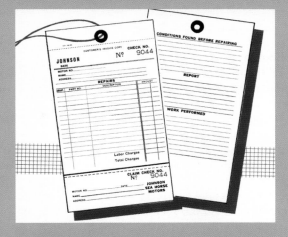

Johnson suggested that its circa 1953 dealers have tags like these printed to ensure the archiving of accurate and orderly information about each motor that enters the shop. A collector might customize them to better manage and maintain his or her hobby outboard menagerie. Space should be provided on the tags for brief notes regarding best fuel mixture, how well the engine last performed, and planned maintenance.

A LONG WINTER'S NAP

There's something deceptive about summer that gives many of us the feeling it'll leave gently. But all of a sudden the boating season passes and idle outboards, particularly in colder climates, become vulnerable to storage damage. To ensure their vintage motors' safe storage, enthusiasts should be sure that all water is drained from the water jackets, lines, and lower-unit gearcase. Some buffs take these precautions:

Kicker Tips 6.5

To Choke or Starve, *That* Is the Controversy

It's not good to leave fuel in the carburetor during motor storage, but should one close the fuel valve or pull the remote fuel hose connector in order to run the outboard out of gas at the end of every use? Proponents like this policy because it ensures a clean, dry carb and fuel system never in jeopardy of leaking or getting gummed up. Contrarians remind outboarders that, in two-cycle terms, when you run a motor out of gas, you're also depriving it of oil. One of this legion probably coined the mantra, "A choke stop protects your motor!" The wisdom there relates to the choke-flooded powerhead getting a mini bath in a protective splash of gas and oil. Both approaches make sense, depending on the classic motor, boater, and how soon the cruising will resume.

Mice and other small critters love to build homes in old outboards. Because mouse houses and the like don't feature modern plumbing, waste goes right to the bottom of the nest and then starts corroding motor parts. This nice original-condition, early-1960s Johnson was stored fully shrouded, but mice still found a way in. Removal of the leaves, twigs, pine needles, and other stuff revealed blistered paint, rust, and corroded metal underneath. The moral of the story is to regularly inspect your old outboards for any signs of such shenanigans.

• Tip and jiggle the motor to coax out remaining cooling water. If used in saltwater, flush with fresh water.

• On motors with accessible water lines, loosen them to let any trapped water escape. It's vital to rid the to-be-stored motor of all moisture.

• Open the gearcase drain screw to allow exit of water that bypassed the lower-unit grease seals. The seal can be replaced and gearcase grease or oil refilled at this time as well.

• For complete assurance that the gearcase is water-free, remove the gearcase cap through which the propeller shaft protrudes. Put this in a plastic grocery bag and hang it onto the steering handle to await re-assembly the following spring.

• Drain fuel tank, lines, and carburetor. Run the motor dry during the final moments of the season's last outing. This is also a good time to clean the carb sediment bowl (if applicable) and fuel screen or filtration.

• Remove sparkplugs, squirt a couple teaspoons of oil into each sparkplug hole, and then rotate the flywheel. This gives the piston(s) and cylinder(s) a protective coating.

• "Fogging" the motor offers greater rust protection. With the motor running, fogging oil can be sprayed into the carburetor. A few seconds of operation with this sticky lube being sucked into the powerhead does a nice job of fending off the harmful effects of moisture during storage.

• Using a lightly oiled rag, wipe the motor to give it a protective antirust coating. Fiberglass or plastic shrouding can be waxed. Cover motor with a sheet or tarp that'll keep away dust but won't trap moisture.

GETTING BACK ON THE WATER

As quickly as cold weather arrives, it'll disappear, even if it's suddenly gone for just one day in March. When that happens, many old-motor buffs feel the call of the water. And if a convenient rowboat is part of the picture, the decision to fire up a classic outboard can be fast made with a determined smile. When this happens to me, I usually find myself rowing back to shore for lack of having done several things best attended to before casting off the bowlines.

• Don't use last season's fuel mix. Some folks swear by the value of a previous year's gas, more than a few end up swearing at it.

• Check for spark (in each cylinder). This simple procedure, as described in Chapter 4, is also an opportunity to blow out (simply via the pistons moving in the cylinders) any excess oil from winter storage and to be sure the plugs are clean and correctly gapped. (See the owner's manual or *The Old Outboard Book* appendix.)

• Inspect the ignition points. If any point contacts are dirty or corroded, clean them with an emery board (nail file), a piece of sandpaper, or by sliding a piece of index card between the two points while keeping the points tight against the paper with a bit of finger pressure. Use a feeler gauge to determine whether the point gap setting is as recommended by the maker.

• Be certain that the lower-unit gearcase is fully greased and that related port screws are secure. It's also wise to check whether or not rattle-prone screws, nuts, bolts, and the flywheel nut are tight.

Adjusting the needle valve settings for optimum combustion at the three major running ranges (slow, medium or start, and fast) should keep your classic humming efficiently, whether you're trolling, cruising, or racing around.

Some of the early auto-start outboards, including this circa 1953 Evinrude Big Twin 25, didn't have an alternator/generator function to recharge the battery. Consequently, battery life was finite. Most early electric-start motors have 6-volt systems. Batteries should be properly stowed, with terminals covered, for passenger safety.

• Gas up with fresh fuel; the oil can be 50 years old as long as it's never been previously used. I caution against second-hand lubrication, however. A neighbor once mixed into his Sears outboard's diet some free, "experienced" motor oil from his brother-in-law's service station. Wow, did that poor kicker have a squeaky and unhappy life! Almost every now-vintage outboard owner's manual mandates first pouring into a fuel can about half of the gasoline you'll need, shaking this mixture and then adding the oil before introducing the rest of the gas. Finally, this brew was to be shaken prior to pouring into the tank. It may seem like lots of rigamarole, but the process ensures that the oil will get to where it can do its best work, as opposed to lying around at the bottom of the can without being well-bonded to each drop of gas.

• Check for fuel leaks and, if its pin is visible, be sure the carburetor float rises.

• Once underway, don't forget to immediately look for signs that the cooling water is being pumped.

• Now there's time to smooth out the carburetor adjustments and enjoy the ride!

"You forgot something very important in this spring re-launching section," noted a fellow outboarder who glanced at the manuscript proofs. After he pointed to a dented old former tackle box, I remembered the importance of bringing along a basic tool kit on the maiden voyage. Actually, it's a wise idea to pack a small assortment of tools, such as pliers, screwdrivers, and an 8-inch adjustable wrench, for every run. Also, although I hate to jinx any outboard-powered excursion, stow a paddle or oars on board, too.

THE ENVIRONMENTALLY FRIENDLY CLASSIC OUTBOARD

Almost as soon as the first outboard-powered pleasure craft popped along America's waterways, their motors began being referred to by their sound: *putt-putt*. As more and more people worldwide embraced outboarding for both fun and commercial purposes, the endearing name caught on much like *choo-choo* came to indicate a train. Once industry leaders such as Evinrude made motors that anyone, not just the mechanically inclined, could run, they set out to move away from *putt-putt* acoustics. The 1934 Evinrude line was among the earliest to incorporate powerhead shrouding to cut down on a bit more audio output than did the original tin-can muffler systems and exposed powerhead. Two decades later, Johnson spent big ad dollars to tout that it had just done "what boating enthusiasts have dreamed of for years and the whole industry has striven for . . . a *quiet* outboard motor." So impressed was the National Noise Abatement Council that it awarded Johnson a plaque for the "development of a quieter" kicker.

Meanwhile, the Kiekhaefer Corporation, maker of Mercury outboards, beat Detroit to the issue of addressing engine emissions. In the 1960s, Mercury released an information pamphlet titled "Water Pollution and the Marine Engine" in which the firm addressed the then newly salient "national concern about water pollution." While industrial and chemical plants have long been targeted as posing the greatest potential to impact on lakes, rivers, and seas, marine engine use was Merc's focus. The motor maker commissioned tests in its "Lake X" research facility in Florida and on a nearby, largely inaccessible body of water in which no powerboats had previously been run. Mercury's brochure quoted various newspapers that covered the study. "Ten years and three-million gallons of gasoline [and oil] later," summarized the *St. Petersburg Times*, "Florida's unique laboratory lake remains unpolluted . . . Neither Lake X nor Cat Lake were found to contain any organic compounds found in gasoline or oil."

When your boat and classic outboard are beached or docked between outings, be sure there is no leaking fuel. Many old-motor enthusiasts take a few seconds to close the fuel valve or disconnect the non-pressurized fuel-hose connector and then run the engine near the beach until the carburetor is dry. On pressurized remote fuel systems, make certain that the fuel tank cap has been released upon returning to shore so that built-up pressure can't pop a hose and squirt out fuel. When the motor is taken on its final run of the season, "fogging oil" should be sprayed into the carb to give the powerhead internals a protective coat of lubricant. There are also fogger-type products that will help keep piston rings unstuck and eliminate some carbon deposits. Check your local marine dealer or auto parts store for the newest and best suggestions.

Summer rewards of a winter revitalization project well done. A 1949 5-horse Scott-Atwater gets a chance to run again in the hands of a young captain who had spotted it sitting gummy and long-neglected in a garden shed. Its rebirth resulted from judicious cleaning, new sparkplugs, some ignition work, and clearing molasses-like goo out of the fuel system. Even the Scott's pioneer gearshift function was coaxed back into service. Now it gets appropriate seasonal maintenance.

Petro-chemical and electro-mechanical technological advances have pushed engine emission efficiencies even further than those known during the Mercury study. Even though the average old outboard doesn't receive anywhere near the seasonal use of a modern one, it's a good practice to follow contemporary protocols when running a vintage kicker. Here are a few suggestions:

• Test for (on land) and eliminate any fuel leaks. Typically, they're due to loose lines and fittings or a faulty gasket. Sometimes soldered joints are broken or cracked and require attention.

• Try a synthetic oil with biodegradable properties.

• When priming the carburetor or making onboard carb repairs, be sensitive to the fact that a single drop of fuel on the water gives some onlookers the false impression that the environment is being irrevocably harmed.

• Run the carb out of gas at the end of the day.

• Be careful not to spill anything when gassing up or emptying an integral tank's contents back into a fuel can.

• Be sure lower-unit gearcase seals are watertight. This is not only good for the gears, but benefits the environment.

• Keep the muffler intact. Many were the occasions in my youth when, not being able to refit the inside element of a muffler can, or just wanting to test a racing motor, I ran without the silencer. Especially in the early morning or evening, this converted very few neighbors to antique outboarding.

• Caution those near the motor about hot mufflers, spinning parts, and lively (exposed lug-type) sparkplug wires.

• Observe all applicable marine rules, carry a fire extinguisher, don't buzz anyone, and keep wakes to a respectable level.

• When underway, don't be loud or talk about other boaters or say anything about people on the shore. Sound carries great distances on water. And, for some, what you say and how you act represents *every* old-outboarder.

• Always offer a tow into shore to any stranded boater, especially if they have a modern engine or a sailboat. Also, give rides whenever feasible.

Above all, we should use impeccable boating citizenship to continue guiding classic outboarding into the same warm-and-fuzzy harbor of public perception as antique cars, old mahogany inboard boats, biplanes, steam trains, and other transportation-related hobbies. It has been my experience that few people who enjoy being on or near the water can resist at least a passing interest in a nicely running antique outboard that motors (or putt-putts) by. With a friendly wave from the hand not busy at the steering handle, the scene can evoke all of the charm of a chugging Model T in the local Fourth of July parade. That's because it offers contrasts and a window on summers past. When we keep our vintage motors truly fit for the transom and for those on the shore, aboard a nearby sailboat, or in a canoe, it's logical to project that brand of acceptance onto classic outboards . . . no matter if you have only one or a couple hundred.

Other MBI Publishing Company titles of interest:

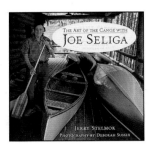

**The Art of the Canoe
with Joe Seliga**
ISBN 0-7603-1241-9

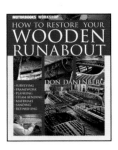

**How to Restore Your
Wooden Runabout**
ISBN 0-7603-1100-5

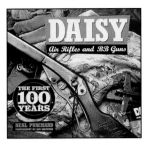

Daisy Air Rifles and BB Guns
ISBN 0-7603-1333-4

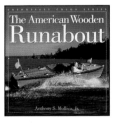

The American Wooden Runabout
ISBN 0-7603-1143-9

Chris-Craft
ISBN 0-7603-0606-0

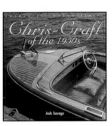

Chris-Craft in the 1950s
ISBN 0-7603-1120-X

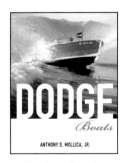

Dodge Boats
ISBN 0-7603-1174-9

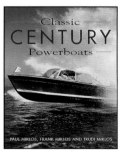

Classic Century Powerboats
ISBN 0-7603-1080-7

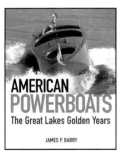

American Powerboats
ISBN 0-7603-1466-7

Find us on the internet at www.motorbooks.com   1-800-826-6600